Debbie,
Thanks for being
so special.
I Love you,
          Debbie
Please use this
often Hope it will
help with questions
you may encounter

# Woman to Woman

# Woman to Woman

## Questions and Answers to today's home problems

Compiled by
Viola Walden

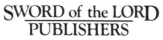
SWORD of the LORD
PUBLISHERS
P.O.BOX 1099, MURFREESBORO, TN 37133

Published 1987 by
Sword of the Lord Publishers

ISBN 0-87398-942-2


Second Printing July, 1987

Printed and Bound in the United States of America

# Introduction

**WHAT A THRILL!**

Hundreds of women singing, "Lord, make me beautiful for thee!" A large auditorium filled with ladies of all ages, sizes, colors and descriptions. They have come from many states and they are laughing, listening, crying, learning, confessing, resolving.

What a thrill—the soft swish of the pages of a thousand Bibles turning in unison as a Scripture passage is read and discussed by the speakers. What a moment—a hushed time of bowed heads, tears, a challenge: "Will you do what God wants you to do?" What a victory as hands are raised, vows made, new courage is taken, and comfort found.

What a prospect—the cars, planes and buses going home—filled with Christian women who have learned what God expects of them; who have learned to find answers in the Bible; who have a new ideal of themselves; who are determined now to pray and find God's will and get His help.

What surprised, happy husbands greet these changed wives— newly determined to make their Christianity work in the home, in life's most intimate and precious relationships, in its hardest challenges— "a new you for a surprised him"!

What joy for the pastors who greet these women—now eager to win souls, to serve God, to live according to God's highest standard. What glorious hope for the future, when mothers, by God's grace, learn how to discipline and love and understand and teach the Bible to their children!

If you have missed a Sword Jubilee, don't despair! These same well-known and loved speakers, who have seen the above results happen to thousands of women, now come—on paper—to help you with YOUR own problem.

In these Sword Jubilees, we sometimes have a "Roundtable" time, a time when the speakers answer questions presented by troubled women. Many of these same questions and answers are gathered together in this volume, to help and bless scores of others. And we have added many others to theirs.

The first section is given entirely to rearing children.

As you mothers have already found out—motherhood is the hardest job a woman can tackle! You don't get a chance to practice ahead of time, nor can you throw away the product if it's a failure! It's just not a job for amateurs, yet all mothers start out as amateurs. These godly women share the things they've already learned.

Wives and mothers, facing certain problems, like to have other wives and mothers tell how they have successfully handled similar circumstances such as: dating, marriage, gossip, working outside the home, coping with pressure, and the like.

That's the purpose of this book. Each speaker who faces these problems has found her own special way to handle them and she does not mind sharing with others her methods and the things she has learned by long experience.

The last section, entitled P.S., gives additional help by great Christian leaders, a doctor, spiritual counselors, a psychologist and other men who have influenced America and the home.

Not only are nearly one hundred questions answered from a Christian point of view, but there is an extensive biographical sketch on each lady represented in this volume. This you will find extremely interesting and helpful.

This is a MUST for every woman. We urge that you see that others get a copy who need the help of this volume!

Viola Walden, Compiler

# Table of Contents

# P.S.

# **B**iographical

Women are strange creatures, aren't we!

Have you ever sat in a church service and listened to a preacher preach his sermon and wondered, *I wish I knew which lady in the choir is his wife. I wonder what she is like. Does she keep a spotless house? Is she a good homemaker? Do they ever fuss and argue? Who handles the discipline of the children? What part does she take in his ministry? How active is she in the church?*

Guests at a Women's Jubilee are always thrilled and sometimes surprised when they meet for the first time Mrs. Jack Hyles, Mrs. Lee Roberson, Mrs. Jackie Dark, Dr. Cathy Rice, the Rice sisters, Mrs. John R. Rice and other speakers who may be on that program. We are not exactly sure what you expect, but you seem to be delighted to find that our great ladies are quite down to earth, humble, everyday people—like us! They strive to serve the Lord, be good wives and mothers, and each leads an active, busy life.

To satisfy your curiosity, here is a short biography on each lady represented in this volume.

**LLOYS McCLURE COOKE** was born on December 20, 1894 in Hood County, Texas.

When she was preparing to go to college for premedical training, a wise evangelist told her father she ought to go to a Christian college, because she was likely to marry the wrong kind of man if she went to a state school.

A day later a surprised Lloys found herself on the campus of Decatur Baptist College.

As in all good love-story fairy tales, the very first person she laid eyes on when she arrived on campus was—you guessed it!—John R. Rice.

John R. Rice entered the army in 1918 and both graduated from Baylor University.

In September of 1921 Lloys and John R. were married and both registered at Southwestern Baptist Theological Seminary at Fort Worth, Texas. Her enrolling with him is probably illustrative of the way her life was to join with his over the years. She was totally involved with every aspect of his ministry.

In the years to come, God blessed the home with six daughters.

In 1932 the family moved to Dallas, where Dr. Rice held several 12- or 13-week revivals. Out of that the Fundamental Baptist Tabernacle was formed. In over six years it grew to some 1700 members—and this in the Depression Days. And because Dr. Rice had seen the power of the written word, he started THE SWORD OF THE LORD and wrote many books.

In the early days of THE SWORD Mrs. Rice sold advertising to help on the expenses. And for many years, she managed the Sword Bookstore, which gave her opportunity to win many souls.

In 1940 Dr. Rice entered full-time evangelism and moved to Wheaton, Illinois, so he could put his daughters through Wheaton College. Too, Illinois would be more the center for his evangelistic ministry.

To show you how much she was part of her husband's work and THE SWORD OF THE LORD, we give this illustration.

In those early years in Wheaton, the Rice home was the office for the paper and the many Sword books. The front hall became the bookstore. In the dining room resided the Graphotype for making stencils of the subscribers, and the Addressograph for addressing labels for the magazine. Crowded into the adjoining sun room were desks for the secretaries, who shared bedrooms with the Rice girls. On the third floor (or attic) were stored the thousands of books waiting to be mailed out.

And every Rice girl had assigned responsibilities in the work, doing whatever needed to be done in order to get the paper out to a growing subscription list.

When asked, "Did you ever resent using your home and girls in this manner?" Mrs. Rice answered, astonished, "Certainly not! It was my ministry, too!"

Yes, this great lady of our generation was totally absorbed in joining her husband in the ministry until God called Dr. Rice to Heaven in 1980.

Now she fulfills the command of Titus 2:4,5 for the older women to teach the younger "how to love their husbands." Though in her nineties, she still travels extensively, charming women all over America. She is an example Christian who knows and loves the Word of God. And she relies on the promises of God for her unusual strength. This great soul winner finds great delight in helping others.

She is a member of Franklin Road Baptist Church, belongs to the local art club and has produced many lovely works of art. Her favorite verse is Psalm 16:11.

There are five living daughters (Grace joined her father in Heaven in 1981), five living sons-in-law (Grace's husband died in 1984), 28 grandchildren and 27 great grandchildren, 20 grandsons- and granddaughters-in-law, a total of 85—"more than Jacob had when he went down to Egypt," she adds!

Back: Jessie, Mary Lloys, Elizabeth, Grace
Front: Joy, Dr. and Mrs. Rice, Joanna

**THE RICE SISTERS** . . . raised wonderful
families while giving three-quarters of their
waking hours to helping others. Mrs. Beka Horton
has said she believes God has preserved this
family as a personal example of biblical teaching
and godly living. She calls the Rice family "the
bluebloods of Christianity today."

## GRACE RICE MACMULLEN (October 22, 1922—October 24, 1981)

Dr. and Mrs. John R. Rice named their firstborn GRACE, taking the name from II Corinthians 8:9. How beautifully she lived up to her name!

She married Allan MacMullen, a Canadian and a Baptist minister who pastored in Idaho, Missouri and Texas. She is the only one of the six who did not meet her husband during student days at Wheaton College.

Many came to know and love Grace. She was a delightful lady, a mother of two adopted children, a creative writer, a musical artist, an imaginative teacher, and an inspiring speaker to women. She was also editor for A.C.E. publications and served as the first editor of *The Joyful Woman*, a popular Christian magazine for ladies. She also assisted her dad with the musical score on several of his songs.

God chose to polish her beautiful character through suffering the last two and a half years of her life with cancer. Those who heard her tender messages to women will never forget the lessons she taught them—submission to the perfect will of God, faith in the unfailing love and goodness of our Saviour, and victory over fear through claiming the promises of God. *God Pried Up My Fingers One by One* was written after she had a mastectomy for cancer.

In her last months, God seemed to particularly inspire Grace's poetry. Her poem, "Someone Special Is Coming Home," gave a note of triumph at her dad's funeral at the end of 1980. Fittingly, her Homegoing service in October the next year was crowned by the reading of her last poem, "What Will I Be Doing on December 18?" written on August 18, when the doctor told her her time was short. No one who knew and loved Grace could be weighed down by sorrow when she pictures herself "doing handsprings and cartwheels" in the meadows of Heaven!

We were privileged to know and love Grace. She told us how to live—but best of all, she showed us how a Christian lady lives and dies to the glory of God.

**MARY LLOYS** is the second Rice daughter.

At Wheaton College, she met Charles (Chuck) Himes and was the first Rice girl to "tie the knot." Together they planned to go to Tibet as missionaries, but ill health prevented the fulfilling of that desire. So Chuck, a Baptist pastor, served churches in Kansas, Wisconsin, Colorado, Tennessee, Nebraska, and is now pastor in Rome, Georgia. Mary Lloys played the piano, sang, taught Sunday school, etc., adding greatly to his ministry everywhere they went. She is now teaching in their church school at Rome, Georgia and is very active in helping ladies through Jubilees and in her own church.

So, Mary has been an evangelist's wife and pastor's wife for more than 35 years.

At one time she wrote the "Kid's Korner" column in THE SWORD OF THE LORD.

Mary is loved and leaned on by just about everybody. Her ear is open to every cry, day or night. She is unusual in her selflessness. She seems to have the remedy for every ill, the comfort for every heavy heart, a bandaid for every sore. I think we can say, as they must have said about Dorcas of New Testament times, "What would we ever do if anything happened to our Mary!"

Soul winning is this Rice daughter's major, and it thrills all who listen to her relate personal experiences in this field. Excellent homemaker, cook, mother and Christian wife in the finest sense of the word.

Five children were born of this union, three girls and two boys. One son, Johnny Himes, named after Grandpa John R. Rice, has been a missionary to Japan for five years.

**ELIZABETH HANDFORD**—we call her "Libby"— is the third Rice daughter and the busy wife of Dr. Walt Handford, pastor of the large Southside Baptist Church, Greenville, South Carolina. The mother of seven, this lady has also found time to teach, edit and author several books for young people: *The Smudged Postmark* (a mystery), *The Fugitive King* (about David) and *The Exiled Prince* (about Daniel). Her books, *Your Clothes Say It for You*, and *Me? Obey Him?* have helped thousands of women. Then another popular title is *Woman in Despair.*

Mrs. Handford took over as editor of *The Joyful Woman* at the death of her sister Grace in late 1981. She teaches a large Bible class of women, and has been featured several times in national meetings, speaking to thousands of wives of pastors and Christian workers. Her counseling ministry has been greatly used of God.

She is also an airplane pilot!

"Libby" was born in Fort Worth, Texas. She attended Wheaton College and majored in English literature, graduating with high honors.

I think her husband's introduction to one of her books is the sweetest tribute she could have:

> With 31 years of watching her life as a dedicated pastor's wife and successful mother of seven children, I can say Libby practices what she preaches. She is the most unselfish person I know. She has deep, abiding biblical convictions and never steps over the line of respect for the authority of her husband. Not always has she agreed with me in everything, but she has never "bucked" any decision I have ever made.... She works hard from early morning until late at night to carry out her duties as wife, mother, author, Sunday school teacher, choir member, and counselor to many women on every kind of subject—from baby care to marriage saving. The message of this book is not theory but advice forged on the anvil of years of experience.

"Libby" is just about the smartest person there is! She knows the Bible as few people do, and has a heart as big as the whole world. She is exciting and inspiring to know, and a continual joy to all who work with her.

*Reminiscence:*

We just knew Libby could do anything! Now we are disillusioned! She confesses there is one thing she is not—a good salesman: "If I had to earn my living selling anything—even refrigerators at the equator—I'd starve.... When a friend asked me to tell about *The Joyful Woman* at her church and about the books I'd written and brought along to sell, I got up and rather timidly said, 'Here are the books. If you like 'em, you can buy 'em.'"

**JESSIE,** the fourth Rice daughter, received her bachelor's degree from Wheaton College and a master's degree from the National College of Education in Chicago.

Jessie, a gifted artist, married Don Sandberg, a gifted musician. After serving for a time as church youth and music leaders, the Sandbergs entered the teaching field on the college level. In 1972 they began teaching music and art at Tennessee Temple University in Chattanooga.

For 27 years SWORD OF THE LORD readers have enjoyed Jessie's "From My Kitchen Window." She now has a new kitchen window! She and Don moved from Chattanooga to Augusta, Georgia, where Don is music director for Southgate Baptist Church and Christian Schools where Rev. Bill Carl Rice is pastor.

She is a lady with many talents: artist, musician, author, speaker, teacher—and on and on. Her several books are very popular; her addresses to women very life-changing. Jessie has made a number of cassette tapes dealing with women's problems. She is a contributing editor to *The Joyful Woman.* In addition, Mrs. Sandberg carries an extensive speaking schedule to women's groups across the country.

Don and Jessie have four children, three boys and one girl, all graduates of Tennessee Temple Schools (now University), and all dedicated to the Lord's work. They have the secret to rearing godly children. And what fond grandparents they are!

**JOANNA RICE RICE.** No, it's not a misprint! Her only given name is Joanna; her maiden name is Rice, and her married name is Rice. She is always having to explain who she is and why she is still a Rice!

She *was* a Rice, one of the six sisters; she *is* a Rice still because she married Billy Carl Rice from Kentucky, no kin.

Bill Rice, Joanna's husband, is pastor of the Southgate Baptist Church in Augusta, Georgia. He is a great soul winner, a gentle and good man and a fine preacher.

Joanna is not only one of the most effective pastor's wives, but she is a soul winner herself, and a mother and homemaker. She teaches in their Christian school, as well as being active in the music ministry and visitation program. You would love her gentle spirit and quiet compassion.

Joanna received her bachelor's degree from Wheaton College and her master's degree from Pensacola Christian College. She is a contributing editor for *The Joyful Woman* and an accomplished musician and soloist. She has a number of tapes for women dealing with the practical problems that women face. She also speaks at many Jubilees and ladies' meetings throughout the year.

Joanna and Bill have four lovely children: Linda, Laurie, Robbie and Bill.


*Reminiscence:*

Joanna had been the baby for six years and she was a little fearful to lose her place of honor in the family. So at Joy's arrival, Dr. Rice jokingly told her, "That little thing can be Mother's baby and you can be Daddy's baby!" So, even as a married woman, with several children of her own, Joanna still signed her letters to him, "Daddy's Baby."

**JOY,** the youngest Rice daughter, was saved when she turned five. She graduated with highest honors from Wheaton College and she, too, married a Baptist preacher, Dr. Roger Martin, who has pastored churches in Kentucky, Oklahoma, Colorado, Missouri, Tennessee, and Georgia. He is now Dean of Tennessee Temple Seminary.

Mrs. Martin was a teacher at Tennessee Temple University for many years before becoming involved in the ministry of *The Joyful Woman* and as head of the Women's Jubilees. She also headed the Concert Choir of T.T.U., heard all over America, and taught large classes in a course called THE PASTOR'S WIFE. And for many years she and her husband Roger, Jessie and her husband Sandy, took groups overseas each summer.

Joy holds a master's degree in fine arts, and is the author of several books.

The Martins have six children, three boys and three girls.

*Reminiscence:*

Her dad, Dr. Rice, wrote about her so sweetly:

When the little one came (six years after the last one) we named her Sarah Joy—Sarah for my beloved mother and Joy because that is exactly what she was! Oh, how she lightened my burdens! I was carrying a load almost insupportable, yet I found myself growing young again playing with my baby! I have had more joy in teaching her, more delight in watching her grow, more fellowship with her, perhaps, than with any of the other five beloved daughters. The others I loved as much, but this one I seemed to need more...."

**CATHY RICE:** Outstanding Christian wife, mother, noted author, lecturer, teacher and businesswoman.

Cathy was brought up in a happy Christian home, one above average in refinement, culture, income and Christian standards.

A tall, skinny preacher named Bill, then 21, met Cathy when he went to hear the "Widner twins" sing on the radio. They became engaged while he was pastor of a small church in Gainesville, Texas.

Cathy literally gave up everything for the man she loved. She lived sacrificially without feeling like a martyr, too.

After working their way through Moody Bible Institute, her preacher husband became a full-time evangelist. During the wonderful years that followed, she had thrown herself wholeheartedly into her husband's ministry, accompanying and helping him in revival campaigns across the states and in many foreign lands, while raising two active boys and two girls, one of them stone deaf.

In addition to their revival ministry, the Rices began what is now the largest missionary work in the world to the deaf, with headquarters on the Bill Rice Ranch in Murfreesboro, Tennessee. They also founded a Bible camp on the Ranch that has the largest weekly attendance of teenagers—both deaf and hearing—of any independent Bible camp in America. When Dr. Bill went to Heaven in 1978, his son, Bill III, took over and the work goes right on, increasing in attendance year by year. Mrs. Rice speaks to hundreds of teenage girls, who come each year, on being 100 percent feminine in dress, actions and outlook.

Along with everything else, she finds time to fly across the nation teaching women on how to be happily married, teaching young women in colleges and Bible schools and teenage girls in Christian schools. No woman in America is better qualified to deal with problems women face. One will be inspired to do right when she hears THE PRINCESS speak.

She is author of the popular book, *The Right Way in Marriage.*

Dr. Jack Hyles has publicly said that he believes Cathy Rice to be one of the twelve greatest women living today. And Hyles-Anderson College bestowed upon her the honorary degree, Doctor of Humanities.

Mrs. Rice's devoted husband, now in Heaven, affectionately called her his "Princess." Yes, this truly was the sweetheart couple of the fundamental Christian world.

**CAROLINE ROBERSON** is the wife of Dr. Lee Roberson. She is vivacious and lovely—a wonderfully sweet helpmeet to her famous husband, who tells her every day that he loves her! No wonder she always looks so happy!

Here are her thoughts about marrying a preacher:

> I said all my young life that when I got old enough, I was not going to marry a preacher, and I didn't intend to. Then I said, *Well, if I should, I don't want any children,* because I felt so sorry for preachers' kids.
>
> But I married the first preacher that came along! I fell in love with him the minute I saw him! He didn't have a chance! He chased me until I caught him! I know he was God's will for my life. We have had 45 years of wonderful married life.
>
> When I married him, he was an evangelist. I thought, *Oh, how wonderful! He's going to travel and I'm going to travel with him.* So I started taking piano lessons. It didn't do a bit of good! My husband said, "Just forget that. You can't sing; I know you can't learn to play the piano—so you just be my wife." And that's been my role, my one-and-only role, for 45 years.
>
> And I take back what I said about not having children. Thank the Lord for our four, all in the Lord's service.

This gracious Southern Belle's wit is showing! Ladies have a good time—and sure learn a lot about Dr. Roberson—when this great lady is talking so down-to-earth to them. While you laugh at her stories, your heart is remembering her message!

She always insists that there is no greater duty pastors' wives can perform than taking care of their husbands.

Mrs. Roberson was saved at age nine, during the preaching of Dr. George W. Truett. She went to Massey Business College and later worked at Prudential Insurance Company in Birmingham, where she met Lee. He was an evangelist, and much of their courtship was by mail.

After the Robersons were married they went to pastor at Fairfield, Alabama, to the First Baptist Church near Birmingham. Dr. Roberson still conducted 55 revivals during their five-year pastorate there. At this time she attended Birmingham Southern College.

Then they moved on to Chattanooga in 1942, where her husband was pastor of Highland Park Baptist Church for more than 40 years, until he resigned in 1983. He also founded Tennessee Temple Schools. And you know the mighty works done in their ministry there. Mrs. Roberson directed the Cradle Roll Department at the church for over 30 years.

Camp Joy in Chattanooga was named in memory of their precious daughter Joy who lived only two months. Ten weeks each summer some 3,000 children, ages 9-14, attend the camp, and many are won to Christ.

Dr. and Mrs. Roberson live on Missionary Ridge in Chattanooga.

Wonderful example, charming personality, Mrs. Roberson answers the questions in this volume from a very sincere and honest heart.

**BEVERLY HYLES,** "first lady of First Baptist Church, Hammond," is usually described as "beautiful," "a model type," or "gorgeous." She is the most perfect lady you will ever know—and looks like she has just stepped out of a bandbox regardless of what kind of work she may have been doing! This "beauty" with her soft Southern accent is an expert counselor, speaker, college teacher, writer, and a fine soloist. She contributes to *Christian Womanhood* magazine and oil paints as a hobby. And this wife of one of America's best-known preachers is also a peerless homemaker and dotes on her four children and nine grandchildren!

Mrs. Hyles has taken part in Sword Women's Jubilees since the beginning in 1978. Always a favorite for her down-to-earth, biblical lessons, this gracious lady gives the women delightful insights into such matters as proper self-esteem, priorities, femininity in appearance; and she tells you how to handle trouble.

Sword Publishers had the privilege of printing her first book, *I Feel Precious to God.*

She and Dr. Hyles have been married for 40 years. She attended East Texas Baptist College.

The Hyleses live in Munster, Indiana.

**GERRI HUTSON**—a more down-to-earth, sweeter, prettier woman you will never meet!

Gerri is the wife of Dr. Curtis Hutson. She is the mother of three daughters and one son, all active in the Lord's vineyard. Two daughters, Sherry and Donna, are married to busy pastors, and son Tony has his own pastorate in Union Springs, Alabama. The youngest, Kay, is a student at Baptist University of America in Decatur, Georgia.

Gerri is a homemaker, cooking delectable meals for her family and the many friends who drop in, whether announced or unannounced. Maintaining the home, looking after her preacher husband and her father, who lives with them, and taking care of her six grandchildren, is her profession. And she does all so well!

What a blessing she is to her own church, Franklin Road Baptist! In charge of hospital and shut-in ministries, she brings a bit of sunshine into the lives of the elderly and sick as she takes her "prescriptions" for health and happiness to numerous hospitals, nursing homes and wherever her shut-ins may reside.

Gerri sings in the choir and also makes herself useful at Franklin Road Christian School.

The Sword, the church, and her family could have no better ambassador!

**BEKA HORTON** is best known as the wife of Dr. Arlin Horton, President and Founder of Pensacola Christian College, Pensacola Christian School, and A BEKA BOOK Publications. Mrs. Horton has had wide and varied experience in the field of teaching. For more than twenty years she taught a weekly Bible class for women as well as the children's television program, "Aunt Beka's Bible Stories." The yearly women's retreat which she entitles "For Women Only" has helped restore many marriages.

Her official function at the present is Vice President for Curriculum and Publishing. She has given the direction and philosophy in developing the A BEKA BOOK textbooks and curriculum which are used not only in Pensacola Christian School but also in Christian day schools throughout America and around the world. These Christian textbooks are used more than any other textbooks in Christian schools.

Mrs. Horton assists her husband in administrative responsibilities at Pensacola Christian College, which enrolls over 1,800 students. She also travels and speaks at the A BEKA BOOK clinics throughout the nation as well as the clinics held in Pensacola.

**APRIL KELLEY** was reared in a godly home in Carthage, Texas. Her dad, Lt. Col. Scott, was a war hero, killed flying bomber raids over Germany in World War II. Her mother, Mrs. Mada Scott, a teacher at Tennessee Temple University, saw all three of her daughters marry preachers. April's husband, Dr. Bob Kelley, is pastor of Franklin Road Baptist Church where most of the Sword of the Lord staff and Bill Rice Ranch workers attend. He says about April:

Aside from thinking April the most beautiful woman I had ever seen, I think the one thing that drew me to her more than anything else was her genuine balance. She was very warm in her personality. On the other hand she had a deep piety that brought her the respect of all the students on campus at Tennessee Temple College. April loves the Word of

God. Many came to her for counseling because of her Scripture memorization and her Bible study. Naturally, since I was a preacher of the Gospel, things clicked in our lives.

I think the one thing that has most enhanced my ministry is her inner strength. April is what I call forever sober. She never panics about anything. Her deep abiding faith is so anchored in the Word of God that she seems never to be frustrated about any crisis that comes. Since I am a preacher of the Gospel, it is always refreshing to me to come home to someone who never worries about anything.

Though she has severe

health problems, she trusts God completely, and does not fret.

April graduated valedictorian of Tennessee Temple Schools in 1963. She is a graduate musician and is accomplished in both piano and voice.

Above everything else, she is a godly mother and an outstanding pastor's wife. She has been greatly used as a speaker to women's groups and has authored many articles in *Christian Womanhood* and *The Joyful Woman.*

Her beautiful spirit is catching. Before Sunday school each Sunday a crowd gathers around her, to tell her their problems, to share their joys—and just to be near her.

For the past several years her body has been racked with crippling multiple sclerosis. Dead legs, numb hands and pain has not stopped her from continuing her motherhood, her writing, her soul winning, nor her music.

A new clinic on the Bill Rice Ranch is dedicated to April and is called APRIL HOUSE.

Dr. and Mrs. Kelley have three girls—Star, Dawn and Daye.

**VIOLA WALDEN** is a Texan. She took Journalism at Wheaton College, Wheaton, Illinois, and Bible at Moody Bible Institute, Chicago. Viola was Dr. John R. Rice's editorial assistant for 46 years: she now holds the same position with Dr. Curtis Hutson.

Because of her column in THE SWORD OF THE LORD, she is known around the world.

Miss Walden assisted Dr. Rice in sixteen tours to Bible Lands and is the author of *With Miss Viola Through Bible Lands, Sword Scrapbook #1 and #2,* and *559 Homemaking Hints.*

She was President of Business and Professional Women's Club in Murfreesboro and was elected their WOMAN OF ACHIEVEMENT in 1967.

She has reviewed and edited hundreds of manuscripts over the years for scores of people, as well as teaching so many Sword workers "the ropes" of the Sword of the Lord ministry.

Miss Walden has a Doctor of Humanity degree from Sioux Empire College in Iowa and a Doctor of Letters Degree from the large Hyles-Anderson College, Hammond, Indiana.

Though Dr. Rice often invited her, Miss Viola never felt comfortable speaking to women's groups, whose problems mostly consisted of children, or a husband! And since she had neither, she did not feel qualified.

However, many sought her advice by letter, single women as well as others. Out of long experience of reading Dr. Rice's mail and seeing his wise answers to a myriad of problems, she was able to lead many a girl down the right path.

We chose three or four of her answers in this book, trusting these will be helpful to many others who may have similar problems.

**MRS. FRANCES HOFFMAN** has served as personal secretary to Dr. Curtis Hutson for over 25 years, first when he was pastor of Forrest Hills Baptist Church in Atlanta, Georgia, and now as President of the Sword of the Lord Foundation and editor of "America's Foremost Revival Publication."

Dr. Hutson relies on her for so many details. She supervises the editorial department, carries a heavy load of dictation, looks after his schedule, helps plan the Holy Land trips and assists in numerous other ways.

"Miss Frances," as she is called, teaches The King's Daughters Ladies Bible Class at Franklin Road Baptist Church in Murfreesboro, Tennessee. She is counselor to ladies all over the country by letter, phone and personal interview. She also travels, speaking in women's conferences. Mrs. Hoffman's messages are warm, instructive, inspiring and motivational.

Married to a fine Christian man, she has two married children and four grandchildren. Both children are in Christian service. Her son is the pastor of the thriving Grace Fellowship Baptist Church in Stone Mountain, Georgia.

**MRS. MARLENE EVANS** is a woman whom God is using to mold and remold the lives of women, young and old alike, to serve the Lord Jesus Christ. She can answer many of the questions that concern Christian women today.

Mrs. Evans received both her Bachelor of Science and her Master of Arts degrees from Bob Jones University. Her Master of Education degree was earned at the University of Tennessee in Chattanooga. She taught orthopedically handicapped and other special classes in the public schools and English and education courses at Tennessee Temple College. At Highland Park Baptist Church she served as Promotional Coordinator of the Sunday school, training union staff member, Sunday school teacher and bus worker.

At Hyles-Anderson College, Mrs. Evans teaches Christian Womanhood, psychology classes, marriage and motherhood classes, and speech. In 1978, she was awarded an honorary Doctor of Humanities degree from Hyles-Anderson College.

She is the editor of CHRISTIAN WOMANHOOD and also Dean of Women at the college. Mrs. Evans prefers to be known as the wife of Dr. Wendell Evans, President of Hyles-Anderson College, mother of Joy (married to Jeff Ryder), David (married to Cathe), and grandmother of

Jordan Lee Ryder.

Here are wonderful commendations by two close friends:

Marlene Evans is not just one of a kind—to me she's an "only"! I've known her for longer than I can believe possible and have always been amazed at her enthusiasm and her ability to make others join in that exciting way she has. I can hear her now saying, "Rejoice in the Lord alway: and again I say, Rejoice!" (Phil. 4:4).

I've seen Marlene when I knew she was suffering physically, yet she had that smile and faith to believe.

Marlene has accomplished much and endeared herself to hundreds of folks and I count myself fortunate to be one of her friends.

—Mrs. Lee Roberson

Marlene Evans is a "builder," not with bricks and stone, but in soft, and *sometimes* hardened, human flesh. So many girls and women have been encouraged to become all they could be because she saw the "hidden gold" glimmering when they didn't know it was there.

Marlene Evans is "medicine." She has such an infectious laughter and an ability to see humor in everything that one can't help but join in and have a merry heart.

Marlene Evans is "courage" wrapped in a lovely woman. Pain has been a constant companion for years along with a bout with dreaded cancer which seemed to give her more perseverance in her many duties.

Marlene Evans is a "teacher" beyond compare. The knowledge she imparts to women and girls seems to come unknowingly and painlessly. Then they realize after a hearty laugh or a "down home" story, they gained new truth and insight.

Marlene Evans is my friend, and I shall be eternally grateful.

—Beverly Hyles

**JACKIE DARK,** wife of Al Dark, former manager of the Oakland A's, who led the team to a World Series victory.

Jackie was, when she met Al, supervisor of airline stewardesses for a certain airline, teaching them well their responsibilities in flight.

Jackie is a dynamic speaker whose life characterizes what she teaches.

You would love the way this beautiful woman dresses, the way she stands, and the way she talks. She knows her Bible, loves it, and uses it in her own life.

When introducing her to the huge crowd of women at the Women's Jubilee in Chattanooga, Mrs. Elizabeth Handford said about her:

I need some heroes I can look up to and feel they really are what they say they are.

I need somebody who lives like she talks.

I need somebody to show me that what she says really works.

Sometimes when we see famous people, like on television, we wonder: Are they just putting on, or are they for real?

The more you listen to Jackie, the more you know that she is genuine and that you can trust her to teach you what you need to know.

She travels with her husband and has a widespread witness. Jackie has a genuine concern, a genuine interest in people.

**JANITH WALLACE** was born into a Baptist home in Baltimore, Maryland, in 1930; she was saved and baptized at age eleven.

Janith met Tom at Kenneth Square, Pennsylvania, at age 16. They were married in 1950 and God called him to preach. In 1952 they moved to Chattanooga. He attended and graduated from Tennessee Temple Schools in two years and nine months.

Dr. Wallace accepted the pastorate of Baptist Bible Church, Elkton, Maryland, in 1954, and in 17 years the church grew from 35 to over 1,100 members. In 1971 the Lord moved them to Beth Haven Baptist Church in Louisville, Kentucky where they saw tremendous blessings.

In 1985 Dr. Wallace gave up the church, and the two are now traveling all over the country holding revival and Bible conference meetings.

They have four children who, with their mates and families, are serving the Lord. Debbie and her husband, Mr. David Hicks, are still at Beth Haven. David is music director at the church. Tom Jr. is an accountant and manager of the Bookstore at Lavon Drive Baptist Church, Garland, Texas. Tim is, at this writing, a fourth-year student at Dallas Theological Seminary. Donna and her husband, Bruce Barton, are at Festus, Missouri.

**TIRRELL VAN GELDEREN** was working for Dr. John R. Rice in Wheaton, Illinois when a young preacher spotted her. The courtship was short. She soon became Mrs. Wayne Van Gelderen.

She has shared with her husband the joys and sorrows of the ministry for the 34 years of their marriage. She has made the parsonage home for their five children. Her three sons are all preachers. The oldest, Wayne, Jr., has accepted a call to the Falls Baptist Church, Menomonee Falls, Wisconsin, after serving with his father at Marquette Manor Baptist Church in Downers Grove, Illinois, for nine years. Jim and his wife are in charge of the Minutemen Evangelistic Team from Bob Jones University. John is an assistant pastor at Hampton Park Baptist Church in

Greenville, South Carolina, while finishing his master's at Bob Jones University. He is also married. Joy has her master's degree in Elementary Education from Bob Jones University and is presently teaching First Grade at Marquette Manor Baptist Academy. Joanna is a junior at Bob Jones University.

Mrs. Van Gelderen is a graduate of Wheaton and Biola. She has served with her husband in pastorates in Florida, Michigan, Colorado, and for the past nineteen years in Illinois. Presently, she teaches a ladies' class in Sunday school and majors on the concerns of Christian women. She is a frequent speaker at ladies' meetings in the area.

Her recent experience with cancer and its treatment has enriched her ministry and helpfulness to women. She is known for her dedication to Bible principles for wives and mothers.

Hear what her husband says about her:

> When I first met my wife-to-be in August of 1951, I was impressed by Tirrell's dedication to Christian service. She appeared to be immersed in her work at the Sword of the Lord and loyal to her boss, Dr. John R. Rice. She was well-trained and knowledgeable concerning the issues of the day. I had just the year before withdrawn from the SBC with my church. In those days few considered this a matter of courage or conviction. Rather, you were looked on as foolish and impulsive, but she immediately rejoiced that this action had been taken.
>
> In the years since our marriage in 1952, my wife has loyally been with me in the battle. On issues that required courage and faith, she was with me regardless of the potential cost. This caused our home to be goal-oriented. This cause was passed to our five children who now stand in the battle beside us.
>
> Instead of bemoaning the pastor's wife's lot of having her husband busy or gone, my wife rejoiced in it and encouraged me. I remember times when at supper I would indicate to the family that perhaps I would not go out to visit. My family would then all volunteer to go and my wife would urge me to go, saying she would go with me—thus forcing me on. This has been great!

**MARCELLA BYERS:** Having a strong desire to serve the Lord, Marcella O'Dell, a West Virginian, attended Bob Jones University to prepare herself for His work and service.

After completing two years at the university, she joined the staff of Sword of the Lord Foundation while it was located at Wheaton, Illinois, working directly under Miss Fairy Shappard of the Advertising Department. How thrilled she was to have part in this ministry and to have constant contact with the Foundation's president, Dr. John R. Rice!

Here she met and married Mr. Alvin Byers in 1961, then a miser bachelor eating his meals from cans!

Born into this union were Robert, Rebecca, Ronald and Ronda (who died after nine days on earth).

Of course, both parents were concerned that their children accept the Lord as their personal Saviour at an early age. "Marcie" had "story time" each day, when she read to them and prayed for them. This created in each an interest in books and in learning. Also, they memorized much Scripture together. Nothing prevented them from going to church every time the doors were open.

All three of the children accepted the Lord at an early age. They made excellent grades in school, graduating with high honors. Robert, who is supervisor of the mail room and subscription department at Sword of the Lord Foundation, graduated from Hyles-Anderson. So did Rebecca, who is now teaching at Franklin Road Christian Schools. Ronny will graduate from the same college in 1989. All three are brilliant young people and all are faithfully serving the Lord. Like parents; like children!

Marcella is still an employee at the Foundation; and all the family attend Franklin Road Baptist. She has a compassionate heart and hand toward the sick and shut-ins, and there is a special soup she makes and delivers to those who need special attention.

Proverbs 31:28 fits her well: "Her children rise up, and call her blessed; her husband also, and he praiseth her." In her tongue is the law of kindness. Her works commend her. Her husband, realizing what he has in "Marcie," praises her.

Not only is she a beautiful, obedient wife, but her every action is Christlike, an example to all who know her.

OBSERVATION:

When someone asked a mother whose children had turned out well, how she had gone about preparing them for usefulness in the Christian life, she replied: "In the morning, when I washed my children's faces, I prayed that they might be cleansed by the Saviour's precious blood; and when I gave them food, that they might be fed by the One who is the Bread of Life. When I started them on the way to school, I asked God to grant them a faith that would be a shining light—ever growing brighter like the rising sun. Finally, when I put them to sleep, I requested that they also might be enfolded in the Saviour's everlasting arms!"

How perfectly that fits our "Marcie"!

# Questions and their Answers

**1** **Q. Do you spank a two-year-old for lying? Our little boy says he is not wet when he is; he says he has already prayed for his food when he hasn't. Also, is saying, "No, Mamma," a spanking offense? And do I spank him for crying and pitching a fit when it is "sleepy" time?**

**A.** MARY LLOYS: First, let's try not to make issues where they do not need to be made. Don't ask a little one if he is wet. He knows it and you know it. (We usually don't spank a two-year-old for being wet.) Don't ask him about anything where the answer is obvious. I might say, "Oh, we forgot to pray," and quietly pray myself, if he seemed to be feeling rebellious.

Many toddlers can be very difficult. If you read the books, you know they talk about the "Terrible Twos."

Yes, it sometimes is a spanking offense, if a tired child can't settle down to sleep. If you say, "You must go to sleep," or, "You must be quiet," and he rebels, a good spanking will—believe it or not—cause him to relax and go to sleep.

I can remember when our son, now a missionary, was about that age. I don't remember what started it, but I said, "You must say, 'I'm sorry.'" He answered back, "No!" I said, "Now wait, Johnny! You must say, 'I'm sorry, Mommy.'" Again he said, "NO, I WON'T!"

It's a good thing there weren't any welfare people around then! After I had spanked him good, I said, "You must say, 'I'm sorry.'" He still said, NO!" His daddy came in; we talked about it, and I kept on spanking.

Finally that little heart broke. Now he sobbed, "Mommy, I'm sorry." We hugged each other. And that was about the last time that child ever needed a spanking. Now he is serving the Lord in Japan.

It does work. It seems drastic to say you could solve things for life at two and a half, but it was almost that way with that child.

I remember spanking our daughter, then thirteen, because she whined and fussed when she was tired. Spanking solved her problem. It makes the child more comfortable, helps him to relax

47

and go to sleep, if that's his or her problem.

So never allow a child to say, "No," or, "I won't," or, "You can't make me."

**A.** ELIZABETH: May I add just one thing about lying. I too would not ask a two-year-old if he were wet. I see no reason to make it easy for him to lie. I wouldn't say, "Did you return thanks for your food?" I would pray with him when it was time to pray and I would change him when he was wet. You will have enough things over which you will have to make an issue, so I wouldn't create an issue.

**2** **Q.** How do you answer the questions of a curious four-year-old about where babies come from? Also her question about human anatomy?

**A.** JANITH WALLACE: The answer is: Keep it simple. Don't be fooled by the writers and teachers of the public school system's "Sex Education Program" into thinking kids need to know many of the specifics of sex at an early age. A long, complicated answer is not usually necessary. Most four-year-olds ask questions about whatever pops into their minds. Usually a quick and simple answer will satisfy, then they will go on with what they are doing.

One simple answer is: "They come from God. God gives babies to mommies and daddies who will love them and take good care of them. Aren't you glad God gave you to Daddy and me?" By asking a question you can change the subject and lead the conversation to another line of thought.

I may be old-fashioned, but I just don't think it necessary to give a four-year-old a lot of details about how we get babies.

**A.** JOANNA: Usually questions that small children ask can be very simply answered. We adults often assume children are asking deep moral questions when they may be asking one simple fact.

When my oldest daughter was four she asked me to show her

how to be saved. I very foolishly sat down with my Bible and went through the entire "Romans Road" with her. Of course she didn't understand a lot of what I told her and she appeared disinterested. When I suggested we talk about it later when she was older, she exclaimed, "But why can't I just ask Jesus to come into my heart and forgive all my sins right now!" She was right and that's exactly what we did; twenty-six years later she still knows she trusted Christ that day and she and her husband serve the Lord full-time in a Christian school.

When small children ask about sex, they usually want to know general facts, not intimate details, as we might think. It seems best to simply answer the questions they ask, matter-of-factly, with the understanding that sex is a very sacred matter and not something to be joked about or discussed in a silly way with friends. Children can be encouraged to come to Mom or Dad with further questions with the assurance they will be told what they need to know.

It seems perfectly proper to give the correct name for different parts of the human anatomy. A mother might say, "There are some private parts we don't talk about in public," and give the proper name when asked.


## 3 Q. How do you teach babies or a small child to behave in church?

A. MRS. JOHN R. RICE: Personally I felt a great responsibility to train my own little ones. My husband, being an evangelist, made it where we were much of the time in revivals. I insisted on keeping my children by my side, so I had to learn to control them, and they had to learn to control themselves.

We began at two to three weeks—while they were yet sleeping in their little portable bassinets. I would whisper, "Be quiet; you are in church." I think they understood soon the reverence and quietness of the occasion. I agree with Dr. Hyles that the Holy Spirit knows baby talk. And if you start training your children for the Lord, He is going to give you wisdom and help.

He gave me a special promise—Psalm 16:11, "Thou wilt shew me the path of life: in thy presence is fulness of joy; at thy right hand there are pleasures for evermore." He said He would show me how and would make me very happy in the process. He said that little ones go astray as soon as they be born, speaking lies. So I knew I had to start "as soon as they be born."

My dad and my husband said children do not have to cry. Feed them when they are hungry, change them when they are wet, love them when they are lonely, care for them when they are sick, and paddle them when they are bad. Yes, cuddle them when they need it, and paddle them when they are rebellious.

Babies are people, too. They respond to loving and training. Start early. Be consistent. When you give orders, see that they are obeyed. And fill them with the Word: "God is love"; "Love is of God"; "Children, obey your parents in the Lord, for this is right" (Eph. 6:1; Col. 3:20); "Pray without ceasing," "Pray about everything."

I had a plan, using as a guide five four-letter words. Teach them to *love, obey, work, pray,* and know the *Word.*

Those things children will respond to if lovingly taught.

"Train up a child in the way he should go: and when he is old, he will not depart from it" (Prov. 22:6). God said it—and He never deceives us. Try it!

> **Jesus never fails,**
> **Jesus never fails;**
> **Heaven and earth may pass away**
> **But Jesus never fails.**

Risk Him and do your part. And start with the baby.

**A.** JESSIE: I issued one warning (along with a little heavy pressure on the upper arm!) when one of my little ones disturbed the service. If there was a second offense, I carried him out of the church as quickly and quietly as possible. Then, when I was out of hearing, I lowered the boom!

I suspect that if you are in a different stage of teaching a child church manners, you ought to sit near a door where you can leave with the least disturbance possible.

**A.** JOY: If a toddler is crying or distracting others, then the child ought to be taken out immediately and not brought back again unless the matter is thoroughly settled. If a mother is training a small child to sit through the services, she should sit in an inconspicuous place where she can slip out quietly. Generally speaking, babies and small toddlers should be put in the church nursery if available, both for the sake of the mother who needs to hear the message, and for those around her. A darling, cooing baby can be every bit as distracting as a whining one!

If an older child misbehaves in church but is not disturbing others, then I would handle it as soon as the service was over.

A wise woman said, "Any discipline which has to be done regularly in public probably indicates that discipline is not being done properly in private."

# 4 Q. Should one leave small children with a babysitter?

**A.** TIRRELL VAN GELDEREN: My feeling is that it is not good to leave them with a babysitter regularly. A mother should be with her children most of the time the first two or three years—perhaps even the first four or five years. When she does have to leave them, it should be with a trusted relative or friend. Much of what she teaches her children can be torn down in the day care centers of our day, as well as in the home of a friend.

We have a day care center in our school and, try as we may to have a "perfect" situation, the children do not always learn good things from the other children there. It is hard to watch all of them all of the time. And sometimes the associations there are not good. A Christian mother has an obligation to see that her children have the right associations and atmosphere.

As for safety, a child can be hurt or even killed when under the care of his parents. However, no one, really no one, will watch the child or look out for his safety like the parent will watch.

**5** Q. **When you spank a two-year-old, how do you keep him from crying on and on?**

A. BEKA HORTON: I'm not sure about a two-year-old, but when I was older, I remember my mother let me cry, then after she figured I had cried enough, she would say, "Now I'm going to keep spanking until you quit crying." It's amazing how fast I could stop crying! When I got much older, I thought, *Well, I just will not cry at all, because I'm going to have to stop anyway.* Then I noticed that Mother would spank me until I did cry! So after a while I learned how to cry just enough, then to hush my crying at just the right time. Maybe as a by-product of it all, I was learning self-control.

**6** Q. **Should the punishment be left to Daddy?**

A. CAROLINE ROBERSON: I've dealt with this in the Cradle Roll and Nursery, where I was superintendent for thirty years. When mothers say to me that they wait until Daddy comes home to do the correcting, that waves a red flag in my face. If I can't control that child, I have no business with him. Leaving it to Dad disrupts the entire family, especially a pastor's family, who have so little time together. If you are going to whip him, whip him before Daddy gets there, then keep still about it. My children used to say, "Kill me, but don't tell Daddy!" They were embarrassed. Then, too, they knew that I could handle the situation.

When our boy was thirteen, I saw him passing notes in church to Dr. Faulkner's boy, and talking back and forth. I said, "I'll come after you, boy, and take you outside." He said, "Don't bother, Mother; you won't see it again!" My children knew I could—and would—handle any situation.

**7** Q.  What if you child insists on going to the altar every Sunday to confess his sins rather than just confessing at home and getting it over with?

A.  BEVERLY HYLES: Perhaps this is embarrassing to you—your child going to the altar. You think people must think, "He must be a terrible kid." I don't believe I would discourage any child from going to the altar. I would never want to quench the Spirit in that child's life. If he feels it necessary to go to the altar Sunday morning, Sunday night, and Wednesday night, I would not discourage him. The time may come when he will be so hard he won't want to go to the altar. It is a good trait when a child feels sensitive to his sin and wants to get on his knees before the Lord and confess it.

**8** Q.  Do you believe that there is such a thing as a hyperactive child?

A.  JOY: Yes, if by hyperactive you mean extremely active. We have six children. Two were extremely active. They were never diagnosed by a doctor as being hyperactive, but a six-month-old knocked the slat off his crib and crawled through four rooms to get to us! He also walked at nine months because he had to be doing things! He's the first baby I weaned early, too. When he nursed, he was constantly moving and he wore me out!

Of course there are hyperactive children. I would be very cautious about embarking upon a drug routine for hyperactive children. I think most children who are extremely active need a great deal of cuddling, and Mother needs a great deal of patience and prayer.

In most cases a lot of things are related to age. That little boy I mentioned above who was extremely active is the one who last night installed our dishwasher. That same little mind that kept him going and figuring out things is the same quality that has given him today a drive in other areas.

Prayer and patience will do much. From a practical viewpoint, a Christian psychiatrist from Chattanooga, Dr. Ross Campbell, has a little book called *How to Really Love Your Child*. While you may not agree with everything he says, he has some wonderful insights we ought to heed. One chapter says one of the very best things for a hyperactive child is cuddling, especially at a stage in his life when he needs reassurance. That book would give you some ideas. But be very cautious about a drug routine unless you have very sound medical advice.

**A.** ELIZABETH: Also, may I add that firm, consistent discipline is helpful!

**A.** JESSIE: We do have to accept the fact that sometimes we do have to invest more in one child than in another. One child may take three times as much attention and care as another. But very often the difficult ones end up being leaders.

**A.** CATHY RICE: I had two very hyperactive children; I had two more who were very, very hyperactive! I also had a very hyperactive husband! So if you want to know how to manage a hyperactive husband and children, get my husband's little booklet, *Love 'Em, Lick 'Em, and Learn 'Em*. It will tell you how to deal with a hyperactive child!

**9** **Q. We have three small children ages three, five and seven. No matter how much or how hard we spank, the rebellion is still there. What do we do now?**

**A.** JANITH WALLACE: You may not realize it, but your problem started a long time ago and has worsened as the years rolled by. When a child is from nine months to a year old he can understand a lot more than most people think, especially about what pleases you and what doesn't. How? By your facial expressions and tone of voice. Somewhere along the line he will decide to do his own thing and put your authority to the test.

Usually a smack on his hand and a "no-no" will suffice, but in a more serious situation, a spanking is in order.

Always spank his bottom, and spank until the child submits to your authority. If the child is stomping his feet, or screaming in a rebellious way, his will has not been broken and you have not succeeded in your disciplining. A good, hard spanking in which the will is broken will head off many others in the future.

As the child grows older, be sure he knows what your rules are and what the punishment is for breaking them. Then above everything else, be consistent in enforcing your rules. The child will soon learn what he can get away with if you are inconsistent.

Always reassure your little one of your love and concern for his actions after administering punishment and let him know that both you and God will forgive him.

**10** Q. Is corporal punishment actually necessary for a child? Are not other methods more modern and more effective? And how soon should we train little ones to obey?

**A.** MRS. JOHN R. RICE: Not if you follow the Bible. Other punishment may be sometimes effective, and certainly there are other essentials to proper child rearing; but spanking has a distinct place, ordained of God, in the discipline and development of children.

When properly administered, a spanking will curb the hot temper of youth, will train little feet in paths of morality and righteousness, and their character will be a pride and joy to both the father and mother who love God and righteousness enough to rear their children according to the Scripture.

Many a life of sin and shame is simply the outgrowth of a life without any discipline, rebuke and reproof. The child who is not punished for sin at home will naturally feel that he can get by with sin in the world. Then the same child will grow into a man without self-control, without a fear of sin, and without a well-developed conscience.

I am sure some of you want to know how soon you should spank a child. As soon as he can well understand the orders given. A child who walks ought to come to us when told to come. Before he is a year old, he ought to lie still at sleep time. And a couple of swats on his behind—the place the Lord provided—can often settle a baby's mind about the dreaded nap.

Susannah Wesley taught her children to fear the switch when they were a year old. Thus the holy lives of these saintly men, John and Charles, grew out of the godly discipline at home.

A consistent policy should be carried out by both parents. Discipline should begin early, and both father and mother should wisely and kindly follow out a simple, godly policy of maintaining obedience regularly, tempering that obedience with mercy and love.

If a spanking must be given, then do it thoroughly, enough to get results: it will save much trouble and heartache later on.

And let me stress that spanking has a place that nothing else can fill in rearing children. The Bible never commands us to make our children stand in the corner, or to get down from the table, or to go to bed early, or to stay in the house when others are out playing ball. The biggest argument for paddling is that the Bible plainly commands it. So when you safely follow the plain commands of the Bible, you know you are on the right track.

Can we rear our children so as to guarantee they will live godly lives? Yes, says Proverbs 22:6—"Train up a child in the way he should go, and when he is old, he will not depart from it." Even when a child is grown and away from home, he will never depart from the training he had as a child, if he was really reared in the way he should go, says this Scripture. Of course, those who are led to Christ in the home and taught the Scriptures and disciplined and nurtured, will make mistakes. But the course of their lives will follow that which they learned at home.

And of great importance is the fact that children properly

reared can easily be won to Christ. We started taking our children to church at two weeks or three weeks, and I began by whispering to my baby, "Be quiet; we are in church." Though the baby does not yet know the English language, yet God helps them as we pray and train. Ours grew up in revival meetings, and all attended the great First Baptist Church of Fort Worth, Texas, with Dr. J. Frank Norris as pastor. I had them by my side. I did not need the service of a nursery. From babyhood they were brought up in the nurture and admonition of the Lord.

Our daughters were saved by the time they were five years of age. We won five of them ourselves and one was saved as she listened to her father's radio message and encouraged by our foster daughter whom we had taken in at age sixteen.

Our children knew that they were dedicated to the Lord by us, and each early surrendered her own life to His service. What a joy and blessing they were in the home!

If you lose your children, you have lost everything. Give careful training and discipline, then watch the Lord as He accepts the offering and makes it turn out to His glory.

The Lord has the answers in His Book of instructions. Take courage and be diligent in the task. He will be there to bless and help you.


# 11 Q. Is it wrong to give a child a play gun?

A. TIRRELL VAN GELDEREN: We never really had a problem with giving our little children play guns. We did not emphasize it that much, nor did they play "Cowboys and Indians" or "Cops and Robbers" that much. A gun to them was just a toy—something that was not that important.

However, for children who see violence in the home and on TV every day, I can see that having the use of a gun, even in a play sense, might not be a good thing. Still, I am not sure how much a play gun has to do with the actual violence children take part in as they grow up. It would seem that the hatred and violence in the home, and perhaps the violent things seen on television, would be the greater forces.

**A.** MISS VIOLA: Here was Dr. Rice's opinion, copied from an article:

"I think this is a matter of judgment where opinions would differ.

"It is natural that boys want toy guns, toy cars, toy tractors, toy railroads, toy airplanes, etc., because they are playthings that remind them of the real thing.

"Some young men will go into the army and will have to learn to use guns; some will be on the police force and have to be familiar with the use of guns. I do not think it is necessarily wrong to let children play with toy guns.

"However, I do believe that the movies and TV often teach violence and bloodshed in a way that does harm. So each father and mother ought to prayerfully consider and make sure that proper reverence for human life, proper kindness and respect for other people, is taught all the time. And if children are given toy guns, they should be taught the proper use of them. To play at being at war with the Indians or to play at being a policeman after robbers, is not wrong, but it could be overdone, of course."

**12** Q. Although Dr. Rice was away much of the time, what could be said about his quality time with his children?

**A.** MRS. JOHN R. RICE: Dr. Rice was, I truly believe, the world's greatest father. He always stressed the importance of family devotions, and we never missed a session. It was our custom to pray and read the Bible together daily. As a family unit, we read it completely through many, many times. Dr. Rice would read two verses and we would go around the table, each reading two verses, until we had read three or four chapters. We would memorize precious verses together, then all would pray and we would talk about any problem. At those times the children were free to ask any questions. Many precious truths were taught them during those hours of family devotions.

Dr. Rice loved dearly each one of our babies. When we brought our firstborn home from the hospital, it was he who gave her her first bath—I was too scared! He got out the little bathtub and bathed her without a qualm.

The first night he took care of her. The next morning when I got up, I saw twelve diapers hanging on a string—twelve changes during that night, and he had made them all!

As we were rearing our six daughters, Dr. Rice's policy was never to bring office work home. He wanted to spend time with each one. He played many sports with them. He taught them golf, bowling, tennis, softball, skating, and other "fun" games.

Dinner at our home was always like a great big party. And Christmas was like a revival! Whatever it was that we talked about, we were always very excited and happy just being together.

**13** Q. In this day when the HEW is taking children out of homes for just slapping a child, many have said we will have to quit spanking, that we must find another method of discipline. Do you agree? As I see it, this is the only biblical method.

A. CATHY RICE: If I lived in a community where I felt I was going to be put in prison because I disciplined my child, then I would forget job, home and everything else and move out to the sticks where I could do what the Bible tells me to do.

A. JESSIE: Did you know this is getting to be a greater problem every day? It's going to affect all of us sooner or later in some way.

One thing Christian parents can and must do is to make sure that when you discipline, you do it the right way. Somebody has suggested that you don't do it with the windows open. Don't spank a child in the wrong way nor in the wrong place. And make sure that you're under control when you spank.

There is some child abuse and I'm afraid that sometimes even Christians abuse a child and say, "We're doing it in a biblical way." You are *not* doing it a biblical way if a child has bruises on his body somewhere other than on his little behind, or if you snatch a child's arm out of its socket, or slap a child across the face, or box his ears. All that indicates is that you are out of control.

Because Christian parents do take a stand on discipline, we have a responsibility to make sure we are doing it the biblical way.

**14** Q. If a parent tells a child he or she can't attend church for whatever reason, what should that child's reaction be? Doesn't God want us ALL in the house of worship?

A. BEKA HORTON: As a daughter whose mother was not yet saved, I wanted to go to church after I had yielded my life to God. In fact I lived from one week to the next just for church, especially for the Sunday night youth group. This was my great joy since all week long I was not with Christians; therefore, I wanted to be with Christians at church.

On Sunday evening, Mother would say to me (at that time I was a senior in high school), "You can't go to church because you have to catch a bus after dark, and it's not safe to be out on the street corners alone at night." That would really hurt because I wanted to go to church so badly.

Sometimes I was tempted to think: *God wants me to go to church. Mother says I can't go. I'll do what God says.* But then I remembered, *No, God didn't say I had to go to church that Sunday night.* So I said, "Okay, Lord, in Your Word you tell me to honor and obey my parents. That's Your Word, so I'll do what Mother says and stay home tonight."

Though it hurt not to be able to go to the youth group and church, I'd sit by the radio, listen to Charles Fuller's Old-Fashioned Revival Hour and have my own little service with the Lord. Then during the next week I'd pray, "God make Mother willing to let me go next Sunday evening. Lord, You work on her heart."

Like all teenagers that age, I didn't exactly ask her if I could go. Rather, I'd say, "Mother, it's about time I get ready to go to church this evening," and hold my breath waiting for her answer. Often, she'd say, "Well, I don't like your going, but I guess you can." Out the door I'd go, thanking the Lord for answering my prayer that week!

## 15 Q. What do you do when your children quarrel and fight? And why do they quarrel?

A. TIRRELL VAN GELDEREN: Sibling rivalry is natural. However, rivalry to the extent of fighting and always being at odds is not healthy nor good. Children are going to fight, true! BUT—they need to learn to love each other, care for one another, and Mother needs to teach them how to share and love to the extent of wanting the best for the other.

Early in life my husband saw that his younger brother had more natural ability than he. So Wayne was willing, though he was the older of the two, to put his brother first, to let him have the limelight. And he truly enjoyed his brother's success. As a result, my husband has had a blessed ministry.

The answer is not to be referee but to teach our children to love their brothers and sisters to the point of being glad for their accomplishments over their own. Children need to learn to rejoice in the good things that happen to their brothers and sisters, and to learn to share. Learning this and being a part of making another happy is a very important attribute in life.

Sometimes fighting is just an attempt to get the attention or approval of Mother and/or Daddy; so we need to pay attention to each one's need and do our best to meet that need.

**A.** GRACE: Sometimes someone will say to my mother, Mrs. John R. Rice, "Did your children fight when they were little? They seem to love each other so much now—have they always been that way?"

And she may say (with memory dimmed by time and a lot of love), "Yes, they have always loved each other. No, my children got along well together. They played happily together, and they didn't fight."

That makes us sound awfully nice, and it is true that we loved each other dearly then and we love each other dearly now. It is also true that in the total picture, we weren't allowed to fight and bicker incessantly, and that there were sore punishments for arguments that continued. But it is not very helpful to leave the impression that in a Christian home automatically everyone is kind and sweet and loving and unselfish, without any temptation to quarreling and disagreements. Just like every other Christian virtue, harmony in the home comes about only when there is constant effort and teaching and sometimes punishment and sometimes reward.

Why do children quarrel? Because they are human and are by nature selfish and thoughtless and self-centered, because, in short, they are sinners! Even saved sinners still think of themselves first, unless they have been carefully trained not to do so. People who live together, grownups or children, find their greatest temptations to sin in their close relationships. Even love does not prevent arguments and quarrels; only determination and wisdom and God's power can enable people to live together and get along well together.

There can be peace and harmony in the home only when this is the expressed goal of the grownups in the home. The example set by the father and mother will go a long way towards demonstrating the Christian grace of getting along with other people. Certainly children are not going to learn to be kind to each other in a home where the grownups are continually cutting each other down and fighting each to have his own way.

A good place to begin, then, is for husband and wife to agree that there will be no quarrels between them; that they will demonstrate God's grace in their lives. A wife's example is especially important, for she gets to demonstrate the submissiveness that children are required to have. Her sweet attitude, her refraining from argument, and her giving in when she cannot have what she wants, will all be effective object lessons to the child who must learn obedience.

Peace in the home should be a stated standard, not screamed at the top of the lungs when everything is topsy-turvy and in upheaval, but planned and discussed and insisted upon.

**A.** MARY LLOYS: Children are born quarreling. It is in their sinful nature they inherited. But good parents don't have to allow it to continue. In fact, we have an obligation to the Lord to stop it. Now the Scripture says, "Let brotherly love continue" (Heb. 13:1) and, "Love one another" (Rom. 13:8); but the mere stating of these doesn't create love nor solve the truculence inherent in every little body.

Probably the first way you can help your children not to quarrel is to set a good example. If you and your husband quietly settle your disagreements without argument and quarreling, then Junior will get the idea that yelling at his brother is not acceptable behavior. Perhaps nothing helps prevent quarreling more than the right attitudes, based on the Word of God. If your family regularly reads the Bible together and the children hear the Bible instructions, the stage is set for getting along together.

Of course, when an argument starts, it sometimes isn't enough just to say, "Don't fight, children." Usually it is unwise to say to the one who hit first, for example, "You were a bad boy." Perhaps that innocent-eyed little girl provoked him unmercifully. Usually one needs to find out the whole story before condemning either. Sometimes Sissy will say, "Mommy, George hit me and I didn't do a thing to him." When George is questioned, he may first agree that she didn't do anything to him, but "she pestered me by calling me names, or making faces," for example. Then a wise mother may see that the seemingly innocent victim really provoked the situation just to get her brother in trouble.

So when we stop an argument, the first thing we do is to say, "You must be quiet and we will find out what the problem is."

When both are perfectly quiet, then one at a time may tell what happened. I find it necessary to insist that one be quiet while the other tells his version, or you never find out the true story, and an argument results in trying to solve the argument!

When the facts are clear, it is easy. We simply decide what is right, state it, and see that the argument stops.

The key to preventing quarrels is found in Ephesians 4:32, "And be ye kind one to another, tenderhearted, forgiving one another, even as God for Christ's sake hath forgiven you." Why must we forgive those who wrong us? Simply because God forgave us for all our sins! May we teach this great truth to our children.

**16** Q. I have a twelve-year-old boy who seems to have given up. He's making bad grades in school; he does not obey when punished; and his two younger brothers seem to be following in the same footsteps.

A. BEVERLY HYLES: From the note given me, it seems the mother is trying to correct according to the Bible. But because this has not changed the behavior, my first thought is, *They are crying out for something.* Maybe these preacher's children are crying for a little more time with Dad. Or perhaps it is a cry for more attention. I would have to know the circumstances in the home to fully advise. Think about it. Is there some way Dad could have a special time every week with his boys, especially with his twelve-year-old?

Boys do need a dad. Moms cannot take the place of a man in the home. Somehow this note struck me as just a cry for attention. Perhaps it isn't. It may be you need to pay more attention to what the Bible says about spanking and correcting. Be sure you are doing things right.

**17** Q. **Mrs. Rice, our twelve-year-old son has no respect for me or my husband. We have disciplined him some. Could you at this late date give us some advice?**

A. MRS. JOHN R. RICE: You have asked a hard question. The Book says children "go astray as soon as they be born, speaking lies," so we need to start immediately training them, even as you start training a pet when it is little. A baby can soon learn what "NO" means. Besides, the Lord is there to help you. Dr. Hyles says the Holy Spirit knows "baby talk." I believe it.

Now the son does not respect you and his father. Hebrews 12:9 says, "We have had fathers of our flesh which corrected us, and we gave them reverence. . . ."

Now you and your husband will need to apologize to your son because you did not chasten him when he went astray, and you will have to begin a new way of life. He will have to be chastened with a switch or with his father's belt if he does not obey instantly.

A father's voice has great authority, and he will have to be ready to enforce with chastening.

I admired so much a son-in-law who loved his children so tenderly but backed his word with a paddle or a belt. I remember how a fourteen-year-old son dallied when he was told to mow the lawn. Finally his dad took off his belt and used it properly. The boy hurried to the task and finished it speedily, then came back to his dad and said, "Thank you, Dad. I wish you had done it long ago." That boy gave his father reverence.

Now you will have to let your son know you require instant obedience and that if he does not give it, there will be a penalty. Pray with him but keep your word. Love requires it. Read with him Hebrews 12:5-11. It will be good both for you and for him, and the dear Lord will help you. As you demand instant obedience, the reverence will come. "A child left to himself bringeth his mother to shame," says Proverbs 29:15. And we read in verse 17, "Correct thy son, and he shall give thee rest."

Love, pray and punish according to God's Holy Book (Prov. 23:13).

You, too, set a good example in the way you obey your husband and reverence him (Eph. 5:33).

"Train up a child in the way he should go: and when he is old, he will not depart from it" (Prov. 22:6).


**18** Q. Our child seems to be so involved in good things—piano lessons, youth activities, ensembles, homework, and basketball—that there's no time for learning to cook, or sew, or do any chores at home. What do you do in such a case?

A. JOY: We Rice girls grew up doing all these things. We all worked at Sword of the Lord office until we were out of college. It is true we took music lessons; there were always revivals to go to, and other things to do. That problem we faced regularly.

It means that you will have to change the times of some designated jobs. If your son has late basketball practice, give him an early morning responsibility. If there is any change in schedule, make it very clear too that if he cannot do his job, he trades with somebody else who can. Each one needs to learn to work, needs to have responsibilities. Certain jobs every child ought to do anyway, like making his own bed and picking up after himself. There are ways, of course. May the dear Lord help you find them.

A. CATHY RICE: No child is going to want to work. None of us really like work. I'd rather ride horses than wash dishes. I'd rather ride on a bicycle or play games or do something else than clean house.

A child is going to try to find an excuse to keep out of work: "I've got basketball practice." "I've got to study," or something else is important to him which he thinks needs done, when it is work time.

I'm reminded of when Pete, my youngest child, was a senior in high school. My husband was in Ohio in a revival meeting. He called me and said, "I want you to come up and spend the weekend with me." This was a Friday. He said, "Now when Pete gets home today, tell him that he is to saddle his horse Saturday morning, go to the back of the Ranch and bring up all the cattle because next week when I get home I'm going to doctor all the sick ones, cut off the horns that need to be cut off and put brands on the ones that need to be branded."

Wouldn't you think Pete would be just thrilled to death to get to be a cowboy? No. He was raised on a ranch. He had been doing that ever since he was five years old.

So when Pete came home from school, I said, "Pete, I'm leaving in the morning to go to Ohio to be with your dad. You're to get up early in the morning, saddle your horse, go to the back of the Ranch and drive up all the cattle."

Do you know what Pete said, "Aw, Mother. Do I have to? I was going to play basketball all day tomorrow."

I said, "Yes, Pete, you have to."

Pete said, "I wish I lived in town. All the boys in town have to do is mow the lawn and carry out the trash, but I have to work hard all day long."

I said, "That's enough, Pete, no more." So I left and went to Ohio.

When I got to Ohio, my husband had another engagement, so a couple and their teenage boy met me at the airport.

This boy said, "You live on a ranch?"

"Yes, I do."

"Have you got boys?"

"Yes, two."

"Are they cowboys?"

"Yes, they are cowboys."

"Oh, boy! Isn't that wonderful? I wish I lived on a ranch! All I do is carry out the trash and mow the lawn!"

I said, "It sure is too bad you and Pete can't trade places."

You see, children don't want to work. You have to teach them; you have to make them work.

**A.** GRACE: This may not be behind the question we have been discussing, but it implies that the school is teaching your children a certain number of things to do and their dad wants them to do certain other things. Now: what do we as parents feel this child ought to be spending his time on?

You and your husband need to make the choice: "What does he need to know in order to be the kind of person we want him to be?" It should include some active things, some sports.

You make the decision whether your girl is going to learn to sew or to be a cheerleader. You, the parents, make the decision whether she's going to do jobs around the house, or whether she chooses piano lessons or something else. In other words, you talk it over; then when you tell her what she's going to do, it will not be: "But the teacher says so-and-so" or, "But Dad says so-and-so." That is how you settle that.

It certainly ought to include cooperation in the home, some home chores. Children need to learn to do things in the home. You decide together which things at school are important.

# 19 Q. Should we "bribe" children to come to Sunday school?

**A.** MISS VIOLA: You know what—you have asked a dilly of a question! The fact is, there simply isn't any one answer—except that we ought to do everything in the spirit of I Corinthians 10:31: "Whether therefore ye eat, or drink, or whatsoever ye do, do all to the glory of God."

There is often a fine line between that which is good and fitting and that which is silly, shallow and foolish. None of us are wise enough to always know just what that line is.

It may be that D. L. Moody was the gentleman who started doing things for children in order to entice them to Sunday school. Moody bought a pony and gave rides to children who would promise to be in Sunday school next Sunday! One result of this was that he built a great Sunday school of over one thousand boys and girls.

Surely Moody was right to get children to Sunday school by giving them pony rides. What harm is done when a church sends a bus after children and serves them cookies on the way to Sunday school? It seems good—not bad—to give a child a pen or some other inexpensive gift if he is in church on a certain Sunday. Or pick up hamburgers at McDonald's before you bus them homeward.

What we do should depend upon what is fitting and upon our motives.

Once Mrs. John R. Rice was in a church where the first three or four front rows of pews were empty. This grieved this lovely lady. "It seems to me," she said, "there ought to be some way of getting those seats filled with people. If nothing else, I'd find a bunch of kids and give each a quarter apiece to come and sit in those seats!"

Don't throw up your hands in horror at this! This great woman has probably won more people to Christ than nine-tenths of the preachers we know. Wouldn't you, too, rather invest a quarter in a youngster anytime than to have him out in the streets on Sunday morning? So, should we give youngsters a prize or award—something to entice them to Sunday school? You bet! When we get a score of children to come to Sunday school by awarding them a pencil, a hamburger, a glass of chocolate milk, consider it money well spent.

I remember hearing dear Dr. Bill Rice say something like this: "Some of you will feel this is not the 'spiritual' way to go about it. If you feel that you ought not give a child a Hershey bar or hamburger in order to entice him to Sunday school, then—if I were you—I wouldn't do it. As for me—after asking God for wisdom I think I might look the Lord in the face and say, 'Heavenly Father, I'm trying to win these children and, at this time, this is the best way I know to get them there.' And then

I would pass out the Hershey bars or hamburgers!"

You have your pastor to account to, so do not cause trouble. However, I don't see how a good pastor wishing to reach the lost could object.

**20** Q. If when children get to be teenagers they become rebellious, rude and disobedient, what are we to do about it?

A. CATHY RICE: We had four children—two daughters and two sons. Then we adopted a rebel deaf boy when he was fourteen years old. He hated everybody. He was hateful and ornery. He had been put out of the Tennessee School for the Deaf, and they were going to take him to a reform school, but he wrote on a piece of paper, "I want to go and see a man named Bill Rice who loves the deaf."

They investigated and found out who Bill Rice was and where he was. So Ronnie was brought to us. We were asked if we would keep him. My husband said, "We'll take him for one week and see what we can do with him." So we took him for one week and we still have him. He is thirty-four now.

This rebel didn't know what it was to be obedient. He had always lived the way he wanted to. He ate like an animal. I thought, *How are we going to work with this boy who just doesn't know anything! How will Bible standards work on him?* But they did. We had strong discipline. We loved him, but we punished him and we made him do right.

You ought to hear Ronnie today tell how, when he would sit down to eat and would reach out for something we would slap his hand. "Mother would slap my hand and say, 'You eat right!'"

Today Ronnie is a fine Christian, a very useful preacher to the deaf. He is just proof of what the Lord can do if you use what the Bible says use.

**21** Q. Why do some Christian kids stay true in a wicked world, while others go astray?

A. JOANNA: My Robbie commented one afternoon when he got home from school, "Mom, you forgot something in my lunch this morning." You see, every morning when I packed his lunch, I wrote a little note on his napkin: "I love you," or "I'll be praying for you—have a good day." But that particular morning I thought, *I'll bet he doesn't pay a bit of attention to those notes.* So I didn't write a note, and Robbie missed it!

You see, Robbie needed my tangible encouragement. I sent him off with plenty of good, nourishing food but I needed to help shield him from the temptations of Satan!

Did you ever wonder how Moses' mother prepared him for the inevitable time when he would take his place in the wicked, idolatrous court of the Egyptian Pharaoh? What made it so he later chose rather "to suffer affliction with the people of God, than to enjoy the pleasures of sin for a season" (Heb. 11:25)?

What about the parents of Daniel, Shadrach, Meshach, and Abed-nego? Did they consciously work at getting their sons ready to withstand temptation and sin in the great land of Babylon as captives, slaves to ungodly rulers?

What was it that made it so "Daniel purposed in his heart that he would not defile himself . . ." (Dan. 1:8)?

What made it so the three young Jewish men, even when threatened with a fiery death, could say, "We will not serve thy gods, nor worship the golden image" (Dan. 3:18)?

And what can parents do to help their children come through their daily walk in a dirty world?

At the top of the list would have to be the Word of God in the home. Deuteronomy 6:7-9 tells us we are to "teach them diligently unto thy children, and [thou shalt] talk of them when thou sittest in thine house, and when thou walkest by the way, and when thou liest down, and when thou risest up. And thou shalt bind them for a sign upon thine hand, and they shall be as frontlets between thine eyes. And thou shalt write them upon the posts of thy house, and on thy gates." We are to continually talk about the Word of God, apply its principles to every situation, and have it constantly before us.

Next, it is important that our children receive the spiritual instruction they need at church. Deuteronomy 31:12 and 13 indicates this by saying, "Gather the people together, men, and women, and children, and thy stranger that is within thy gates, that they may hear, and that they may learn, and fear the Lord your God, and observe to do all the words of this law: And that their children, which have not known any thing, may hear, and learn to fear the Lord your God. . . . "

The Word of God is so important in our lives that God commanded each king of Israel to "write him a copy of this law in a book . . . And it shall be with him, and he shall read therein all the days of his life: that he may learn to fear the Lord his God, to keep all the words of this law and these statutes, to do them."

Practically, how do we do these things?

First, make sure the family reads the Bible together. Then make sure your home looks like a Christian home and that your family as well as guests are reminded of God's Word as they relax or work. It may be no more than a favorite portion of Scripture. And see that your children spend some time each day reading the Bible for themselves. You may need to provide a daily reading schedule and require it of your older children until they develop the love and desire for it on their own.

What else can Christian parents do? Never neglect prayer. Every mother's thought about her children should also be a prayer for them.

Don't be afraid to have rules and to enforce them. Rather, you ought to be afraid NOT to have rules. Be sure your children understand the laws of sowing and reaping. Be consistent; what you promise, deliver. Check up to be sure they are obeying. Be the right kind of example in faithfulness, in right attitudes, and in support of God's leadership in the home, at school, at work, and in the church. Your attitude toward husband, teacher, boss, pastor, and youth leader, will influence your children more than you dream it will!

Be very careful about television, music and reading materials in the home. What you teach can be completely torn down here, unless you are careful and diligent.

How can we send our children out into the world, prepared to withstand the temptations and snares of Satan? "Above all, taking the shield of faith, wherewith ye shall be able to quench all the fiery darts of the wicked. And take the helmet of salvation, and the sword of the Spirit, which is the word of God" (Eph. 6:16,17).

## 22 Q. Can you, Mrs. Hutson, give us some rules for rearing good children?

**A.** GERRI HUTSON: 1. Parents should begin early to discipline their children. "He that spareth his rod hateth his son . . . " (Prov. 13:24). You know, we think the opposite is true—that if you spank a child, you don't love him. Sometimes well-meaning friends say, "That child will think you don't love him," but that is not true. He *will* think you love him if you do it right. " . . .but he that loveth him chasteneth him betimes" (Prov. 13:24). The word "betimes" literally means "*early*." Our four children learned very early that they should obey what we said.

2. Discipline should be consistent. If you spank a child for something today and let him get by with something worse tomorrow, this confuses him. And it is really unfair to the child. He never knows when he is going to get a spanking and when he is not.

Teaching is a two-way street. You are only teaching when the child is learning. And whatever the child has learned is what you have taught.

3. Parents should be good examples to their children. You can make the child do right even if you do wrong, but the ideal way is that you do what you want him to do.

4. Associate love with correction. "For whom the Lord loveth he chasteneth, and scourgeth every son whom he receiveth" (Heb. 12:6). God chastens because He loves us, and He does it for our own good. Associate love with correction. Tell the child you love him and because you love him, you must spank him when he disobeys; that you are correcting him for his own good. It is not enough to simply say, "I love you." Communicate love.

5. Comfort the child after correction to reassure acceptance. Usually when the child is corrected, until his will is broken, he will seek reassurance of the parent's love. He should not be sent to his room after punishment since this indicates rejection and is also double punishment.

It is important that the one giving the correction also give the comfort. Sometimes the child may seem to reject the comfort in order to get it from the other parent, but the one giving the correction should give the comfort.

Children may be comforted by the presence and attention of the parent as well as by words and hugs.

**23** **Q. Mrs. Rice, you have six talented daughters. How did you and Dr. Rice develop their talents?**

**A. MRS. JOHN R. RICE:** We made sure that our girls were afforded the opportunity to take music lessons. I supervised their practicing. We always had two pianos in our home while our girls were growing up; we also had an accordion, two violins, and several other musical instruments.

Today they all play the piano beautifully; they all sing specials and lead choirs. All teach in Christian schools. All but one are authors. They learned this from example. That was a way of life for them. We made it a priority to help them develop their talents and we gave them the opportunity to pursue their interests.

**24** Q. Can you suggest some good family summer projects?

A. JOANNA: First, plan projects to fit the needs of each individual. Analyze the needs of each, then prayerfully look for creative projects to meet those needs—physical, mental, spiritual and emotional.

The Scripture admonishes us to "give attendance to reading" and to "study to shew [ourselves] . . . approved unto God."

One valuable project could be *regular trips to your local library*. You might make a chart with each child's name, a space across the top to list each library book brought home, and space for a colored foil star for each book read. At the end of the summer, that long line of stars will be impressive. One summer my husband paid our boys a modest sum for each 13-page booklet they read from the Christian Hall of Fame Series, and we found it worth every penny invested. One year our girls read every book in the series, *Biographies for Young Americans*.

Another project to stretch the mind is to *memorize Scripture and other great literature*. The end result is fantastic. One way to make Scripture memory work doubly profitable is to choose Scriptures to meet special emotional needs of each. You might have a study of all the verses you can find on fear, anger, lying, or pride, using a good Bible concordance, then set out to memorize these Scriptures.

A family member with a weight problem can *plan nourishing but low-calorie meals as a project, or experiment with low-calorie desserts.* Another could plan times for family exercise—morning jogging, jumping rope and moderate calisthenics. Let each set his own weight-loss goal and award special recognition to the most successful each week.

*Beautifying yard and/or house could be another physical project, or learning to sew, becoming proficient in a sport, building a tool house, or training a pet.*

*A weekly family activity is very special.* How about a Saturday morning cookout with each member manning his own "hobo" stove? Individual stoves made from one large can per person (such as a tomato juice can) with an opening cut in the bottom to feed your fire and a small hole near the top of the back for a chimney, will provide lots of fun. Each member scouts his own "firewood" (twigs and sticks) and when the fire is burning nicely, he fries his bacon slices on the bare top of his "stove." When the bacon is cooked to his liking he removes it to his plate, breaks his eggs into the hot bacon grease. Bread can be toasted on a stick at the opening in front or grilled on top of the stove. With juice and hot coffee or cocoa from a thermos, breakfast is ready to be served! After breakfast, just throw away your paper plates and toss your "stove" into the garbage can and you are ready for some exciting sets of tennis or whatever sport suits your family.

*What about choosing one of your missionary families and make it a year-long project* to communicate with them and inform them of family and church happenings throughout the year? Not only will your missionaries be grateful, but you will build a missionary spirit into your children! You might want to climax the summer with "Christmas in August," and mail an assortment of small items and love gifts wrapped in Christmas paper to your "family missionary."

Best of all, *plan for family soul winning.* Let each parent take turns going visiting with a different child each week. One of the best blessings I have had as a mother came as a result of taking my baby and three little ones to visit a new neighbor. After leading her to the Lord, I happily led my little brood home and had the joy of hearing my four-year-old say, "Mommy, could I do what that lady did—could I ask Jesus to come into my heart, too?" "He that winneth souls is wise" (Prov. 11:30).

Sit down now and make a list. Share it with your husband. Get ideas from your children. Pray about it. Then expect this summer to be forever remembered as "that GREAT summer."

## 25 Q. How can a mother build character in her children?

A. FRANCES HOFFMAN: Experts tell us the first six years of a child's life are the most important. If at all possible, Mother should be at home with her child during this decisive time.

*Character is built by correction.* Children come into this world with a sin nature. When they do something wrong, they must be lovingly corrected. This must be done consistently. Every time the child does something wrong, he must be corrected. That means sometimes he must be spanked, and sometimes he must be told or shown the right way, according to the offense.

*Character is built by teaching.* Isaiah 28:10 says, "For precept must be upon precept, precept upon precept; line upon line, line upon line; here a little, and there a little." I think this means that you must spend quiet time with the child every day. You must talk to the child quietly and calmly, instructing him or her on everything from how to put a doll baby to sleep to how to fix a toy airplane.

Read to the child; sing to him; memorize Scripture with him every day. Teach your child to pray. Instruct him on how to trust Christ as Saviour. Teach him good manners, how to care for his body. Everything he needs to know ought to be taught at Mother's knee.

*We build character when we encourage.* A wise woman builds her house. And one of the best builders for a child is to have someone who believes in him. Brag on your child when he does a good job. Make him believe he can accomplish anything if he gives it a try. Lift him up when he fails, and encourage him to try again.

*But the most important way to build character is by your own example.* Anything you want your children to do, you must do yourself. If you want your girls to have a quiet and a meek spirit, you must have that same spirit. If you want them to be good housekeepers and good cooks, you have to set the example by doing it first. If you want them to be obedient wives, you must be an obedient wife. If you want your boys to be diligent workers, then work yourself. If you want your children to love Jesus, then you must love Him.

Good character is not built accidentally but on purpose.

## 26 Q. What is your philosophy of disciplining children?

**A.** MRS. JOHN R. RICE: Dr. Rice taught me that obedience is not obedience if it is not *instant* obedience. First, we trained our children to obey, then a second principle we observed was that they were not allowed to fret, cry or pout.

Soon after they were born, each child was taught what the word "no" meant. We started training them immediately. Dr. Rice believed in spanking. And if I saw a child needed a spanking, I did it myself. I did not like to, but I knew that to do wrong gets one in trouble and I was afraid for them to do wrong, so I spanked to protect them.

Children need to know what is expected of them. They like a Code of Conduct. They like to know that it does not pay to do wrong. No one needs to "beat" a child, but you must make him understand. There are times when you must whip hard enough to let that wrongdoer know that what he did was very wrong.

But you get most of that settled in the first five or six years. After that, you won't have to do much spanking. Only two of our girls required this treatment after they were teenagers and as far as I know, none of our six ever rebelled against us.

Dr. Rice and I felt it was our responsibility to be in charge of our girls until they were married; and so we were. When Grace, our oldest, was ready for college, we moved our location to Wheaton, Illinois, so she could attend Wheaton College. In fact, all six graduated from Wheaton. And all but two have their master's.

## 27 Q. What are some ways to teach Bible principles to children?

A. MARCELLA BYERS: As situations come up in everyday life, teach Bible verses that fit the situation. One my own mother taught me was, "Withdraw thy foot from thy neighbour's house; lest he be weary of thee, and so hate thee" (Prov. 25:17). She would quote this verse to me when I would beg to go visit my best friend too often. I used it with my children.

"Thou shalt not steal" had a whole lot more meaning to one of our sons after one specific lesson. One day he took a grape from a shelf in the grocery store and ate it. When I realized what he had done, I stressed the fact that that was stealing and very wrong. I made him tell the clerk what he had done and give her a few cents to pay for the grape. You may think that was such a little thing that it would not matter. But honesty is not a little thing and children need to be taught to be honest in all things, big and little.

One time our daughter went through an especially difficult time of having bad dreams and being afraid at night. A verse that helped her during that time was, "When thou liest down, thou shalt not be afraid: yea, thou shalt lie down, and thy sleep shall be sweet" (Prov. 3:24).

When our children wanted to get involved in disagreements not really of their own concern, my husband would quote, "He that passeth by, and meddleth with strife belonging not to him, is like one that taketh a dog by the ears" (Prov. 26:17).

Another time my husband gave the children a true-life example of, "a soft answer turneth away wrath . . ." (Prov. 15:1). We had rented a garden spot and there was no fence or marker to separate it from the adjoining garden. After we had the garden plowed, the owner of the other garden came out and told us we had taken some of his garden space. He was very angry. With a soft answer, my husband turned away the man's wrath and we had a friend.

One very important principle to teach, of course, is obedience.

My husband says, "Don't say 'no' until you mean 'no,' then give it your whole attention." Our children learned early that when Daddy said, "No," he meant, "No," and no amount of begging or crying would change that. Teach them to obey by not allowing disobedience to go unpunished.

Here is a verse for us parents: "Except the Lord build the house, they labour in vain that build it . . ." (Ps. 127:1). We need to pray earnestly for the Lord's help and guidance in teaching our children, for unless He builds our house, our labour is truly in vain.

## 28 Q. What material or books would you recommend for family devotions?

**A.** MARCELLA BYERS: In our devotions we used only the Bible. We each read a verse until the chapter was completed. As soon as our children learned to read they joined in. Then each of us would pray.

Daddy would often give some explanation or lesson from the chapter and answer any questions the children or I would have.

Sometimes I would make up questions from the chapter to ask. We would have a variety of questions, such as: fill in the blank, true or false, etc. Our children enjoyed the quizzes.

*Egermeier's Bible Storybook* is a very good one. The stories are short and interestingly written. There are questions and answers that go along with each story. I used this book for bedtime stories before the children went to bed. This book would be good to use for devotions along with the Bible, but in my opinion the Bible itself is best, and even a small child can learn much.

## 29 Q. When you Rice girls were young, did you ever rebel against your parents, smoke, drink, or dance? Or did you all see eye to eye? Did you ever fight or argue about doctrine?

**A.** GRACE: None of us ever embarked on a program

of rebellion. None of us ever said, "I've had it with this. I'm not going to live by your standards."

As teenagers, none of us ever drank, nor even tasted it. It was very embarrassing once when Dr. Bob Jones, Sr., eating lunch with us, asked, "Have any of you ever tasted a cigarette?" I had to say, "Yes, once." My cousin and I were in the back seat of a car. I was just dying to know what a cigarette tasted like, but I didn't want to smoke. He handed me his and I went "puff! puff! " and that was it. I don't believe any of the others were that naughty! We never smoked, we never drank, nor even thought of doing such a thing.

Rebellious? There were days when we didn't want to wash the dishes. There were days when we didn't want to wear our hair the way we had to. But we loved the Lord and we wanted to please Him, so we got over our rebellion—sometimes with a little help from a belt!

We weren't perfect children. The important thing is, we were taught early that it is God who is judging us, not the people around us, not the people in church who may criticize us. We knew we had to face God for what we did. Mother and Daddy did teach us to love the Lord and to want to please Him in everything—not because there were rules, but because He has done so much for us. Oh, we loved Jesus!

**A.** MARY LLOYS: We were taught, "The eyes of the Lord are in every place, beholding the evil and the good" (Prov. 15:3). We did work to please Mother and Daddy. We did—and still do—what is right, but the basic thing was that we wanted to please the Lord. The Lord saw what we did when Mother and Daddy did not.

It is also true that we sometimes fought: you didn't know we were normal! We disagreed and we acted like all kids. We rarely disagree now, but we do have big discussions. We probably don't disagree on a single major doctrine, but we'll discuss some individual passages of Scripture and take different views. There has never been a time when we didn't love spending time together. Those were precious days, precious hours, precious moments!

**A.** JESSIE: We will have to admit that we did fight and argue. One sort of unusual thing about our family was that at mealtime this was encouraged. Some don't understand how we could be so dogmatic when we were raised to be submissive.

But the one thing Daddy did, which may be hard for some to understand, is that our mealtimes were kind of a forum. Sometimes we would quote poetry, or sing, or discuss all kinds of things—political, or theological, or whatever.

Very often Daddy would ask for an opinion by posing a question. Sometimes this brought on very hot and heavy discussions. If we have developed opinionated ideas, perhaps that is where they originated.

**A.** JOY: For your encouragement, you have to remember that children are going to fuss at one particular age. I'm sure that at one point in my young life my sisters thought I was a spoiled brat. They even told me I was! But they didn't always know my heart. There were times when we didn't understand each other.

But the beautiful thing was: the older we got, the closer we got, and the more we understood. There are definitely no differences between us now.

It is so wonderful to know that you love one another, that you will stand up for each other no matter what happens. That's the beautiful thing about Christian love. The more we grow in the Lord, the more we are able to love each other just like we are.

**30** **Q. I am a schoolteacher, unmarried, already in my twenties, who desires a home. How do I pray? I was engaged to an unsaved man but broke the engagement, knowing it was not right to marry a non-Christian. Why doesn't the Lord give me someone else?**

**A.** MISS VIOLA: I have a deep sense of fellowship

with you in your effort to find the will of God. God made us male and female. There is certainly nothing wrong in a man or woman having a normal desire for the destiny to which they were created. It is not wrong to want a home and someone to love and work with and for. But a Christian needs to be very careful not to run ahead of God in this serious matter, this decision which must last for a lifetime.

The Bible principle which should control our actions and thoughts on this is that given in I Corinthians 7:27,28: "Art thou bound unto a wife? seek not to be loosed. Art thou loosed from a wife? seek not a wife. But and if thou marry, thou hast not sinned.... Nevertheless such shall have trouble in the flesh...."

It is not a sin to marry, but it brings trouble in the flesh, says this verse. One who marries does well, but one who marries not does better.

If God gives you a mate and the love is there, and the marriage is clearly not against His will, then you have a right to marry. But if God has not given you one to love and marry, then I ask that you be content in the state in which you find yourself. The same principle holds for both man and woman.

A good woman wants a home, a husband and, where this is possible, children. At the same time, there are many special blessings for those who stay single. I ask you to read I Corinthians 7:32-38. If one can be content single, there is a greater opportunity for service. I speak from long experience as a single woman. One has less distractions, says the Scripture. Marriage in most cases hinders the singleness of heart that is best for serving Christ.

Many women have a subconscious sense of need for security, and it seems more marry for that reason than for any other. So I believe you should analyze and identify this urge for security.

In the first place, it is misleading. Marriage does not give security. Especially is this so in these days. Only God can give us security, happiness, and the comfort in many loving friends.

Did you know that most marriages bring as much misery as

happiness? If you were married, you would have to submit to your husband, and most women find that is not easy nor pleasant. If you were rebellious, there would be constant quarreling and unhappiness. And if there were children, these things would bring heartache to them also.

It seems there is more happiness for one who is content to stay single. Thousands of Christian women would have been far happier teaching school, or working a computer, or being a good secretary, than married to the man they are now married to.

I just recently read a sad report: *"One half of all marriages in America end in divorce."* We thought it was bad when it was two out of six or seven, or at most, two out of five. But now it is half and half! To half the married people in America, marriage is a miserable failure. And many of those who stay together simply live in an armed truce.

No, happiness does not come from marriage alone but from doing right, from being in God's will, from being adjusted to one's duty.

Yes, continue praying for Mr. Right to come along—but pray with this in mind: I will be content with whatever the will of God is for me. Prayer is not a way of making God do what we want, but of finding His will and getting or having what it is His will to give us.

I congratulate you on your decision not to marry the unconverted friend whom you greatly respected. You will surely have a reward in Heaven because you made an honest sacrifice for Jesus' sake and you chose what was right, though your heart yearned for love and human happiness. Don't you think God sometimes gives us a chance to make a choice that would honor Him, even when the choice was not intended as a real opportunity for marriage? I know that one day you will be very glad that you had that chance to marry but did not take it because it was against God's will and plan. Now you know this much about yourself better than before—that when tempted, you still will try to please God, whatever the cost.

I am sure you are trusting the Lord about the incident which occurred. He meant it for good and meant to put you on record, as He did Abraham in the case of offering Isaac. Now you can thank Him for that evidence of His care over you and that He gave you grace to do right.

And if God does not give you someone else worthy of your love and devotion, then you can thank Him that He has reserved you for Himself and take it that He does not want you to be distracted with the love and care of a husband. At first that may seem a loss, but in the end, it will be your great gain.

And this leads me to say that I feel certain that some of the unmarried young women who work for us at Sword of the Lord Foundation are happier, far happier, than most married women; and certainly they do far more good than they could do if they were married.

I hope you will become absorbed more and more in your ministry to children as a teacher, in your church and in your own personal soul winning.

Dear friend, don't think me careless about the deep hurt in your heart. Believe me, I see that this matter is very real and deep, and I want to help you as a true sister in Christ and as your friend. I want the best God has for you.

In closing, I beseech you—to humbly wait on God and do not fret. You have no time limit on one of the most important decisions of your life. The Lord has something sweet and good for you. So be as expectant as possible. Tell Him all your heart, then claim His promises.


**31** Q. I am fifteen and want to get married. I am now serious with a nineteen-year-old fellow who is unsaved. I am a Christian. Can you advise me about my life?

A. MISS VIOLA: You are fifteen, will not be sixteen until August, yet you long to get married, and the boy is unsaved. You ask me what you should do.

I hope you will listen and heed my advice.

You ought not marry anybody when you are just fifteen, and

never a man who is unsaved. So right off, I strongly advise that you immediately break any relationship, engagement or promise to this unsaved fellow since such a union would bring only misery and heartache.

First, let's discuss your age, then we will talk about your dating this unsaved boy.

No girl is ready to marry at age fifteen. You may have a woman's body but not a woman's head, nor a woman's experience. You may be old enough to fall in love, but you are not old enough to make a good wife, nor are you old enough to have good judgment about raising a family. You haven't even finished high school, my child!

A girl your age is even required by law to have the consent of her parents before she can obtain a marriage license! The law knows one so young cannot wisely decide such an important matter on her own. And did you know that people everywhere regard you not old enough to vote, not old enough to hold any office, not old enough to sign a note and have it legally binding? You are still considered a child. So how could you think a fifteen-year-old is old enough to make the wisest decision of her life!

And the truth is, most girls your age who get married are soon divorced since they don't have much to build a home on. Young people are simply attracted sexually to each other, infatuated by the opposite sex but not ready for the heavy responsibilities that go with marriage and home. Real love—the kind that lasts—must be based on character and a certain agreement in mind and heart on great principles, not on sex attraction.

Then, were you to marry now and become a mother at, say seventeen, you are still not mature enough to know how to raise a child.

So by all means, just give up all thoughts of marrying SOON.

But even more serious than your age is that the boy is unsaved. Since you are a Christian, then God says all your special friends should be Christians, both boys and girls. No Christian has any business dating an unsaved boy. Second Corinthians 6:14-18 warns you not to yoke yourself up with an unbeliever. To be married for a lifetime to one who is against Christ—how could any Christian be happy that way? You may think, *Well, he'll get saved later.* Thousands of others have thought that—only to suffer a broken heart, a family of lost children following their unsaved daddy. They had misery, quarrels—and their own Christian life never amounted to anything because of their yoking up with children of the Devil. That is wrong, dead wrong, and the Bible forbids it. And if you go against the plain command of God in this and tie yourself up with one who is unsaved, you will certainly feel God's wrath, and suffer much for it.

Now to my last point. Again I say—wait! Have fellowship with *Christians* from your church, both girls and boys. Enjoy a good time. Don't rush into marriage. In due season, perhaps God will grant you the desire of your heart.

Go ahead and get your education—and dead sure make up your mind you will marry only a Christian, somebody in the will of God, then you can expect God to bless you.

This may not be what you want to hear, but nevertheless it is true.

And please let me hear from you again. This time I hope it will be good news.

## 32 Q. How does one go about finding a God-given mate?

**A.** APRIL KELLEY: Probably this is the most frequently-asked question of Christian singles today, and rightly so. Next to your own salvation and living for Jesus there is nothing more important than marrying in the will of God. He wants each of His children to be happy, and He is very capable of giving us a "partner for life" at just the exact time He knows we need one.

Since I can only speak with authority from personal experience on this subject, I am going to pinpoint some important guidelines the Lord used to lead me to "Mr. Right."

1. Have personal devotions every day and stay close to Jesus.

2. Put first things first. Give yourself to the Lord every day and let Him make you a blessing to others. (Don't always be thinking about, "What will I get?" but about, "What can I give?")

3. Keep your life pure and clean.

4. Set your standards high concerning the type person you date.

5. Have lots of good Christian friends. "He that hath friends must show himself friendly."

6. Make much of the promises of God in your life. "But my God shall supply all your need according to his riches in glory by Christ Jesus." "Wait on the Lord: be of good courage, and he shall strengthen thine heart: wait, I say, on the Lord."

7. In today's world there is much more emphasis on the outward appearance than there is on inward beauty. Let's keep ourselves attractive *inside* as well as outside!

Marriage is a lifetime proposition. As we live our lives every day, we can trust God to lead us to the exact person He has planned for us to marry. Let *Him* do the matchmaking!

"But seek ye first the kingdom of God, and his righteousness; and all these things shall be added unto you."

## 33 Q. Should young people always have a chaperone? Did the Rice girls ever date alone?

**A. GRACE:** People don't believe us when we tell them no, but it is true. We had a firm rule: you do not date without a chaperone in the car. We could be in the living room alone, but not even there if there could be a temptation.

The longer I live, the more I see how wise that is. I know all the things they say: "Don't you trust us?" I heard Beverly Hyles answer that one: "No! I don't even trust myself!"

So if you love your girl and your boy, see that they are not left alone. Boys need protection as well as girls. Have you seen teenage girls lately? Their actions? The way they dress? Their forwardness?

**A.** BEKA HORTON: Grace, may I interrupt? I didn't grow up in a Christian home like you Rice girls, but my mother was very strict. My husband-to-be visited me in my home during a college Christmas holiday, but Mother discreetly never allowed a situation for us to be together alone at home. Though she did not have a Christian background, she had enough sense to know it wasn't good to allow us to be tempted. The only time we were alone in the living room was after my parents retired for the evening. Their room was down the hall, and the door was left half open. With their room darkened, I couldn't tell but that they were watching. Now, I realize that this made for very healthy behavior on our part.

Could it be that we are too lenient today toward our young people, and thus we see the tragic results in their behavior.

## 34 Q. Am I really in love? How can I be sure this is the one for me?

**A.** JOY: Real love, contrary to what is frequently portrayed in romantic books and movies, is not just an overwhelming emotion that will hit you out of the blue—BANG! . . . "I'm in love. This is the man I want to spend the rest of my life with. WHEE! Isn't it marvelous?"

No, love is "compounded of both the head and the heart." While it definitely involves one's emotions, real love is based on a choice, a commitment that you make.

My dad used to say to each of us six Rice girls when we were being courted, "You didn't fall in love—you *climbed* in!"

Check your love by the qualities described in I Corinthians 13.

Love that lasts is based upon character and ideals, not merely upon physical attraction.

In his book, *The Home: Courtship, Marriage and Children*, when my dad gives principles for a happy marriage, he asks,

"Young woman, do you love your intended husband because he is strong, brave, sensible? . . . Do you like the way he stands up straight, like his strong body, his kindness to his mother, his gentleness to old people? Are you proud of his Christian character, his faithful, clean life, his ambition and plans for the future? If so, then that is the kind of love upon which happiest marriages are built."

Some of you girls think the worst possible thing that could happen to you would be not to marry. I can tell you something worse—to marry the wrong person! Decide ahead of time the qualities that are really important to you in a husband and do not sacrifice these. To guide your thinking, here are some qualities a Christian girl should look for:

1. *He must be saved* (II Cor. 6:14). No amount of love can overcome the handicap of the "unequal yoke."

2. *He must share your dedication to Christ.* Do you believe the same basic doctrines, share the same convictions? Can you pray together and discuss spiritual matters?

3. *He must be worthy of your respect and confidence.* Is he considered reliable by others? Is he often depressed and negative, or is he stable and cheerful? Does he handle money well?

4. *There must be a freedom to communicate,* to be sincere and open with each other. Can you talk about all sorts of things comfortably? Are there some subjects you must avoid?

5. *There should be many common interests.* The more mutual interests which can be developed, the better. Are your educational and intellectual backgrounds similar? Do you enjoy being with him, no matter what you are doing?

6. *There should be physical attraction.* When you love someone, you are proud of the way he looks. It is normal to want to be close to the one you love, to look forward to his caresses in marriage. The wondrous attraction is a blessing, but becomes a curse when not committed to God and controlled. Remember to be a good example to others, and not do anything that would bring guilt or embarrassment, that would hinder your prayer life or joy in the Lord.

7. *There should be a clear agreement on the permanency of marriage, about intimacy in marriage, about children.* Ideally, both of you should read the same good Christian books on marriage and get wise Christian counsel regarding marriage from your pastor, youth leader, or teacher. This will prevent many future misunderstandings.

8. *Have the blessing of both sets of parents on the marriage.* No matter what anyone says, there is a sense in which you marry not only a man but a whole family—its traditions, culture, economic standards, intellectual viewpoint, spiritual values and even its genetic makeup (physical characteristics and personality). So never disregard the opinion of your parents, even if they are not Christians. Remove all barriers. God will honor this submission (Col. 3:20).

9. *Pray earnestly for God's leading and wait for His assurance that this love is His perfect will* (Ps. 37:4,5,7).

Look before you leap, girls. Love that lasts can be tested. It is worth waiting for.

**A.** JOANNA: Here are ten questions you can ask yourself in determining the answer to this all-important question:

1. Have we dated over a reasonable length of time? (Love takes time!)

2. Do we want to be together and experience good companionship apart from common sexual attraction?

3. Do we have similar interests, enjoy the same kind of activities, like the same kind of people?

4. Do I have a sense of security and trust in the relationship?

5. Is there mutual concern for the needs of each other?

6. Is his mental and spiritual self as attractive to me as his physical charms?

7. Do we have similar values and goals?

8. Do we have a good line of communication between us?

9. How do he and my family relate? Enjoy, endure, or avoid?

10. Do I have peace in my heart when I pray about God's will for my life regarding him?

**35** **Q. If a girl has not kept herself pure before marriage, when she marries should she tell her husband about her tainted past?**

**A.** GRACE: It would not be wise for her to pour out a lot of things about her past. Perhaps it would be all right to say, "I haven't lived as I wish I had, but the Lord has forgiven me," not giving the details unless she gets to the point of not telling the truth.

My sister Libby has dealt with this. Let me ask her to say a word on it.

**A.** ELIZABETH: Two things. One: If a girl is marrying a man whom she does not think loves her like she is, she ought not marry him. Two: I also would say, don't go into details, only say, "I have some regrets about my past relationships." If a man pressed her to tell all the details, then I would say she probably ought not marry him, for he might not have a forgiving spirit.

It's been my impression, in dealing with married couples, that it will be more likely to hurt than to help, to reveal past indiscretions. A man may have a right to know if the girl has some regrets for her past. If he loves her, knowing that, the marriage can be a happy one.

**36** **Q. Please advise me regarding clothes and standards. I have a problem of staying warm in winter. And what is practical to work in around the home?**

**A.** BEVERLY HYLES: I always know when I mention pants that I'm going to get some flack. They are comfortable, I suppose. It seems women just don't want to give them up.

This inquirer says she has a problem staying warm when the

thermostat is turned down to 68°. I guess she thinks that's a good excuse for wearing slacks. But why not surprise your husband and get some real feminine long skirts to wear around the house, or some hostess robes? I bet he'd really like that. And they are real warm. But that wouldn't be very practical to do your work in. You might wear some leotards or even heavy stockings for that. When he's not around to see you, you can look kind of tacky and still be warm.

If pants are wrong one place, they are wrong another place. I know that the Scripture doesn't say, "Thou shalt not wear slacks." But it says, "The woman shall not wear that which pertaineth unto a man. . . " (Deut. 22:5). His clothing today is pants, so I assume that verse means pants.

You wanted to know what to work in. Skirts are very practical once you've gotten used to them. Your problem is, you have worn pants so long and gotten so used to slinging your legs around any old way, you don't know how to move in a skirt. You'll get used to it, believe me.

I've ridden a camel in Egypt in a wide skirt. I've ridden a horse in a wide skirt. I do my yardwork in a skirt. I scrub my toilets in a skirt. And I manage very easily. Mrs. Handford says in her book that when she took a tumble one day, her first words were, "Oh, did my skirt go up?" She was told, "No; you handled it beautifully." Why? Because she was used to skirts. You just need to get used to wearing a skirt. Skirts are comfortable, and can be used in any situation.

**A.** MISS VIOLA: We can always make up some excuse for not doing what is right. A woman may say that pants are warmer, but she never said that when it was not stylish to wear pants. Now women say they are more convenient for gardening and other things; but they never said that until it got to be the style to wear them.

God intends for men and women to dress differently. And it is generally understood that pants are for men and dresses for women. And we know that tight-fitting pants reveal the form more closely than a loose-fitting skirt.

All through the years modest women dressed in skirts which covered their nakedness and they did that while working on the farm, picking cotton, pitching hay and milking cows, and while they took part in sports and did other things they wanted to do.

Pants are conforming to the world, and we Christians should be different by looking different.

Sometimes our Sword girls and the Bill Rice Ranch ladies wear culottes—divided skirts—but I think no one regards divided skirts as masculine.

## 37 Q. Please tell me if I should or should not wear jewelry. I am bothered about this, and what about I Peter 3:3-6?

**A.** MISS VIOLA: If it hurts your conscience to wear jewelry, then don't wear it. But the Bible never says jewelry is wrong, so we must not make rules where the Bible doesn't make them. It does require that a woman not make her jewelry or hair or clothes her real adornment (I Pet. 3:3), but it does not forbid jewelry or braided hair or clothes. It would, however, be wrong for one to be vain about her looks or too much occupied with her looks.

Great women—and some men—of the Bible wore jewelry.

We have reason to believe that Sarah wore jewelry and fine clothes. When Abraham sent after a wife for his son Isaac, the servant gave Rebekah earrings, bracelets, and other jewels of silver and gold. It seems likely some of the jewelry had belonged to Sarah. Surely Abraham would have given jewelry to his wife if to his daughter-in-law. And Sarah is commended in I Peter, and other Christian wives are exhorted to be like her. So if Sarah wore jewelry, then there would be nothing wrong in other women wearing it, would there?

And Rebekah, the bride of Isaac, is a type of those Christians who are the bride of Christ. And she wore jewelry.

God had the high priest in the Old Testament wear a jeweled, golden breastplate and a jeweled mitre.

When John saw Christ in Revelation 1:13, Jesus had on a golden girdle.

Now the outward adorning is not what we are to depend upon. Rather, our adorning is inward—that of a meek and quiet spirit (I Pet. 3:4).

So let us beware of manmade rules by those who criticize others. Real Christianity is not how we look outward but being right in the heart. If a modest amount of inexpensive jewelry offends your friends, then it seems to me they are too critical. However, if those are the kind you associate with, then you should try not to offend them.

Let me also add: Any Christian should be willing to give up anything that God requires. But we will do very great harm if we go to making rules which God doesn't make, and if we go to requiring incidental things, outward things, which the Bible does not require, and think that we please God by living up to certain rules, instead of being Spirit-filled, soul-winning Christians.

I am against worldliness, but we must not make up our own definitions of worldliness.

I would like for beautiful Jackie Dark to further comment on this.

**A.** JACKIE DARK: I will number my thoughts on this for you.

1. Jewelry should compliment, never dominate.

2. Jewelry should always be appropriate: casual with informal and sportswear; tailored with suits; elegant with dress-up dresses and formals.

3. It should never place a doubt in the viewer's mind what sort of woman or girl you are.

4. It should not reflect copying the styles of the worldly or carnal.

5. Fads in jewelry are just that—fads that pass by the scene very quickly, so it is not a wise investment. This is not meant to exclude suitable, inexpensive costume jewelry. Classic

jewelry, such as pearls, are an investment in that which has stood the test of time.

6. No piece of our jewelry should ever make the world doubt whose property we are.

Finally, when in doubt, DON'T!


## 38 Q. Mrs. Hyles, do you approve of make-up, little or much? Some say it is all right, while others disapprove.

A. BEVERLY HYLES: Obviously, I do. I really do not find a particular Scripture that is clear-cut on the matter. I remember as a little girl I watched women of a certain religion who didn't believe in make-up or even color in dress. I was really repelled by their appearance. I remember thinking, *They aren't consistent.* You see, they wore lots of white powder (or it looked very pale) and no other make-up, hair very severe, and usually black or dark clothing. It seemed *to me* that the powder was make-up and their look drew too much attention to themselves. I do not think they glorified God.

I don't like to shop in the generic section of the store because everything is black and white. I am drawn to color.

I do not want to be a "generic" Christian. As much as I can, I want to be in fashion with my make-up, hair, clothing, etc.

This seems to *not* draw undue attention, but gives one a better chance to be a real ambassador for Christ.

In make-up, whether little or more, the key is starting on a clean canvas (your face), and then blending make-up so there are no telltale lines of demarcation: make everything look soft and subdued.

Especially as women grow older, skin color fades, so some blush and fresh lip-color over a soft foundation can be very beautiful. Our God made *everything* beautiful, and being ugly purposely doesn't make us spiritual.

Of course, we must always be aware that the real lasting beauty is from inside and no amount of make-up or Oil of Olay can cover lines of hardness and an ugly spirit.

## 39 Q. What about mixed bathing?

**A.** ELIZABETH: In our family we have always had the rule that boys and girls swim separately. In our church we have no activity where boys and girls swim together. If they go to camp, the boys swim on one lake and the girls on another. Nudity is nudity for whatever excuse, and it can be a real temptation.

When our children were young, we would sometimes take them to a secluded place on a beach where the family could swim together. But even there we insisted that the girls put on cover-ups as soon as they were out of the water. And we did not allow sunbathing on the beach.

**A.** MISS VIOLA: Everyone surely knows that promiscuity has greatly increased over the last decade. And one reason this is so is that modesty has been broken down. Scanty attire has certainly helped endanger the morals of our country.

When a man—young or old—sees the naked flesh of a pretty girl, it is likely to stir passion and lust. Modesty concerning one's body is an essential part of good Christian character. And we don't find modesty in today's bathing suits!

## 40 Q. Does it really matter to God how a woman dresses? Does the Scripture give any guidelines about what kind of clothes godly women and girls should wear?

**A.** JOY MARTIN: Yes, God's Word does deal with women's dress. It is a fascinating Bible study to discover God's principles concerning our clothing.

First, our dress and general appearance should be characterized by *cleanliness*. In Exodus 19, the children of Israel were being prepared to come into God's presence. Notice the instructions God gave to Moses in verse 10: "Go unto the people, and sanctify them to day and to morrow, and let them wash their clothes."

In the Old Testament, to enter into God's presence required outward cleanliness as an important symbol of spiritual cleanliness. But today we do not "come into His presence" if we are saved. Rather, God Himself in the person of the Holy Spirit lives in our bodies. First Corinthians 6:19,20 teaches us that our body is the temple of the Holy Ghost; therefore we are to glorify God in our body, and in our spirit. So our body should be clean and sweet and our clothing fresh and spotless.

Second, our clothing should be distinctively *feminine*. Deuteronomy 22:5: "The woman shall not wear that which pertaineth unto a man, neither shall a man put on a woman's garment; for all that do so are an abomination unto the Lord thy God."

Men and women have different roles, so they are to dress differently. I believe this Scripture also is warning against homosexual practices (which are clearly forbidden in both Old and New Testaments). The New Testament teaches that even the length of hair is to be a definite symbol of masculinity or femininity (I Cor. 11). Clearly, the unisex idea in appearance and action is displeasing to God.

When a girl dresses in a distinctively feminine way, she is saying to the world, "I am delighted to be what God made me; I am glad to be a woman fulfilling God's plan." My Aunt Cathy, Mrs. Bill Rice, says, "I want to be a woman from the top of my head to the tip of my toes." I do, too!

In our culture, the most distinctive womanly apparel is a dress. Unless a man is perverted, he wouldn't be caught dead in a dress! So why not make this basic symbol—a dress—our standard attire!

In the third place, a woman's clothing ought to be *modest*: "that women adorn themselves in modest apparel" (I Tim. 2:9). True modesty begins in the heart with the attitude, "I don't ever want to wear anything that would tempt a man to sin. More than that, I don't want my actions in any way to be suggestive."

In Matthew 5:28 the Lord Jesus makes it clear that sexual

sin begins with a lustful look. So a woman or young lady who deliberately displays her body in such a way that it causes a man to be tempted is also guilty of sin! God designed a man to respond to the sight and touch of a lovely woman. In marriage this response and arousement is a part of God's beautiful plan for expressing love (study the Bible book of The Song of Solomon to see God's design for intimacy in marriage). Therefore, except in the privacy of her home with her husband, a woman ought not to wear clothing which is cut so low at the neck, or so short at the hemline, or so tight across the bustline or hips that even a pure-minded man might be tempted. Let's make sure that our clothing is *modest*!

The fourth Bible principle is that our clothing ought to be appropriate; that is, suitable, or sensible for the occasion. Sometimes we women are pressured by the fads of current fashions to wear inappropriate, even ridiculous clothing. In Titus 2:4 the older women are instructed to teach the younger women to be "sober" or sensible. I'm afraid some of our contemporary fashions are designed to make us look foolish. For example, why do some women wear shoes that hurt their feet and make them "wobble" when they walk? Because they are fashionable! Why do you see women today sometimes wearing a huge shirt (preferably three sizes too big), unbuttoned halfway or off the shoulders, and belted over a full skirt? It is an outfit that is not becoming, not sensible, and not modest—but it is considered "fashionable"! Christian women ought to discover for themselves what is becoming to them—in color, design, material—and not be mindless slaves to fashion.

Appropriate clothing also means that it is suitable for the occasion and the age of the wearer. My navy suit with the pink blouse and dressy navy sandals is fine for church or a ladies luncheon, but it would look ridiculous on the tennis court! For my Saturday game with my husband or teenaged boys I will wear my cotton cord culottes, cut in a modest style, with a knit shirt and white tennis shoes. The elegant formal gown might be perfect for the Christmas banquet, but completely out of place for Wednesday night prayer meeting! The point is, we ought to be sensible and wear clothing appropriate for the occasion, for one's age, and for her size and shape!

The final principle for women's clothing is that it ought to be *beautiful* and becoming. You may say, "Are you sure that is really in the Bible? That sounds awfully worldly to me. I thought if you were really spiritual you should look sort of tacky. Isn't it vain to even think about wearing pretty clothes?"

Many Christian women have come to that false conclusion because of a misunderstanding of Scripture. First Peter 3:3, 4 teaches that our basic adornment, that which makes us truly beautiful, is "inner," not "outer"; it is "the ornament of a meek and quiet spirit" which is of great price. But that does not mean we ought to neglect the outward appearance. While it is true that "God looks on the heart," it is also true that "man looketh on the outward appearance" (I Sam. 16:7). We are daughters of the King of Heaven! "The King's daughter is all glorious within: her clothing is of wrought gold" (Ps. 45:13).

The outstanding example for Christian women is the virtuous woman of Proverbs 31. Notice the description of her apparel: "She maketh herself coverings of tapestry; her clothing is silk and purple." She used fine, beautiful fabrics both in dressing herself and her family and in furnishing her house. Even the colors were important (vss. 21,22); "her household are clothed with scarlet" and "her clothing is . . . purple." This good woman worked hard to make cloth out of wool and flax, and then she went to the extra trouble of making scarlet and purple dyes, obtained in biblical times from plants and seashells. Surely, then, it is proper to give attention to the texture and color and design of fabric.

You see, the Lord Himself gave us the ability to perceive color and to enjoy it. Notice how God describes His clothing of the people of Israel in Ezekiel 16:10-14. He clothed them with "broidered work" and "fine linen" and "silk"; He decked them with bracelets and jewels and earrings and a beautiful crown and their renown "went forth among the heathen for thy beauty: for it was perfect through my comeliness, which I had put upon thee." Then the next verse shows why God rejected Israel: "Thou didst trust in thine own beauty, and playedst the harlot." The sin was not in the beautiful apparel; God Himself gave the lovely garments; the sin was in the wicked heart attitude.

Let us first make sure we have "clean hands and pure hearts," then let us seek to dress beautifully for God. We need not be extravagant and wasteful about clothing, but we ought to know how to spot a bargain and wear becoming clothes.

Next time you are purchasing or making new clothing, you might remember these guidelines: Is it clean, feminine, modest, appropriate, and beautiful? Every day when you are dressing, why not ask yourself, "Will this clothing please the Lord?" And then pray this prayer: "Let the beauty of the Lord our God be upon us" (Ps. 90:17).

—Taken from *The Joyful Woman.*

## 41 Q. What are some practical rules for modesty in clothing?

A. BEVERLY HYLES: Some rules for modesty in clothing could begin by realizing there is clothing that says we are "harlots." See Proverbs 7 where the "strange woman" wore the attire of a harlot.

What is this attire?

1. Anything that exposes too much flesh (shorts, bikinis, halter dresses, etc.)

2. Those things that accentuate the "female parts." Included in this would be low-cut dresses, tight-fitting pants or shorts, tight sweaters or knits. One can be covered but be very sensuous.

I believe we are to dress beautifully as Christian women because we are God's temple (see II Cor. 6:16), which was beautiful and ornate in Solomon's time. We are "priests," and they dressed beautifully and colorfully (see Exod. 28:4-35).

Some things we might ask before we wear a garment are:

1. Would I be pleased to walk with Jesus in this?

2. Is it appropriate so that I do not draw attention to myself?

3. Is it modest? Does it cover enough and fit properly? I believe we can be in fashion except when fashion goes to extremes (miniskirts, etc.)

An ambassador from America is not one who dresses shoddily, smells bad, looks bad. He looks sharp because he represents our great country. We are ambassadors for Christ (II Cor. 5:20), so let's glorify Him in our body, in our clothing, and in our spirit.

## 42 Q. Mrs. Rice, what are the dress codes for the summer activities for the Bill Rice Ranch? And are those codes strictly enforced?

A. CATHY RICE: At the Bill Rice Ranch we are extremely anxious that young men who come to camp look like young men and that young ladies who come to camp look like young ladies. Therefore, we ask the young men who come not to wear skirts; likewise, we do not want any of the young ladies coming to the Bill Rice Ranch wearing trousers!

Since we have a thousand or better attending camp each week, we get young ladies from all across the United States. Though we advertise and have our dress code in our camp folder, we will sometimes have them come with culottes which are not our preference. In other words, the culotte is skimpy when we require a full skirt to the knees and not visibly divided. But, if a young lady comes with only slacks and shorts, this we remedy immediately. We get her dress code culottes so she will not have to be about the Ranch in men's apparel.

We also have separate swim times for the girls and boys. The girls swim first, then the young men. We ask that each wear a robe to and from the pool and that the girls not walk past the boys' dorms on their way to the swimming pool. These rules are strictly enforced.

In our early years, there were those who prophesied that we would never be able to build a camp with these rigid restrictions. But, we have grown year by year and suffer far more from lack of space than from lack of young people.


# 43 Q. How can I witness to an unsaved husband?

A. APRIL KELLEY: Many Christian ladies either marry an unsaved man, and he then accepts the Lord sometime after the two are married, or the man may even refuse to be saved. Both situations are unfortunate, yet God's Word always gives us instruction on how to handle every problem we may face.

Amos 3:3 asks a most important question: "Can two walk together, except they be agreed?" The obvious answer to this question is: "NO."

Yet, over and over in Scripture we are admonished never to give up on the power of God to alter certain circumstances we find ourselves in, no matter how complex they are!

Years ago I had a Christian aunt who was married to an unsaved man. He drank heavily and would never attend church with her and the children. But she faithfully served the Lord, taught Sunday school, and was a cheerful wife and mother. *She daily showed love in the home.* Possibly one of the most valuable works she did was *daily pray* for her husband's salvation. Paul's words held true in I Corinthians 7:14, "For the unbelieving husband is sanctified by the wife." After fifty years of waiting upon God, she saw her dear husband accept the Lord!

That is quite an unusual story, yet it did happen. It can happen to any Christian who determines to be the *best wife* she can possibly be to her unsaved husband.

How can one be that kind of wife? I give my "how" in the list below:

1. Pray secretly and faithfully for her own life to be a blessing to her family.

2. Be kind and loving in the home.

3. Keep the house neat and orderly so her husband will be proud to live there.

4. Show appreciation to him for the way he provides for the family.

5. Guard her tongue (gossip, criticism, fussing).

6. Be faithful to serve the Lord at church as much as her husband will permit. (This point may sound strange, but I think many Christian wives who have unsaved husbands often are too busy in church work while they neglect their husband and wifely duties.)

7. Believe Mark 10:27—"...with God all things are possible."

## 44 Q. You are busy doing the Lord's work but your husband, who claims to be a Christian, does not like to take part in church activities. How can you get him to take spiritual leadership?

**A.** CATHY RICE: First and foremost, you can't change a man! If he's not spiritually minded, you can't force him to be. First Peter tells us that by the way we act, we can win our husbands to the Lord if they aren't saved, or we can bring them back into fellowship with the Lord if they are backslidden. So just be a lovely sweet wife, act like you ought to, and leave it to the Lord to change your husband and make him more spiritual. You can't change him.

**A.** ELIZABETH: May I add one thing to that? Sometimes we say we want our husbands to take the spiritual leadership when we don't really want them to. We go ahead and make our decision, then want them to confirm it. If they don't want to make a decision, then we insist they make one, when they have made a decision by not doing it. Probably we need to back off and let them take the leadership. Most men will not pull it away from us.

**A.** JESSIE: I have found too that you can help a man to take spiritual leadership by expressing your need—not to point out his need and problems but to ask him to help you with yours. For example, if a woman says to her husband, "I feel I'm a

104

failure in this matter. Will you pray right now about my problem?" If a man gets used to having the opportunity of praying with you about your own particular needs, it will encourage him in other situations.

## 45 Q. If a husband won't, may the wife lead in family devotions?

A. GRACE: First, a Christian mother must remember that her life is the most important Christian witness her children can have, and it will have a powerful effect on her husband, too. What she lives may be far more impressive than Scripture verses, at this point.

So perhaps the most important principles about having family devotions if the husband is not willing or able to do so, would be these:

1. Assume that your husband would like to do right about it if he knew how, and assume that if you go about it the right way he will be agreeable.

2. Prepare the way by making time for Bible reading. Get up early so there is no rush, prepare a good breakfast, and have the children ready. Then it will be easy to say, "Since we have a little time now, I thought we could read a few verses from the Bible together. Would you like that?" You might even have a section chosen—just a few verses that are extra good.

3. Be sure that you do not accuse or threaten or embarrass when you try to make plans for family devotions, as these things will make it more difficult for your husband to be willing to have family worship.

4. Don't have too fixed an idea of exactly how a family should go about having Bible reading together. Be flexible and let your husband do it his way, if he will, and avoid being critical of how he does it.

5. If he doesn't want to lead, but wants you to, feel free to go ahead and have family worship together. Be sensitive to his feelings and watch for signals that he is willing to assume more responsibility later.

6. Even if he is not willing for you to have devotions, be sure your personal devotional life is such that your family can be blessed by *your* Bible reading and your walk with the Lord. Ask God daily to show you how to teach the Bible to your children in the time you have together with them.

7. Make it your earnest, daily prayer that God will lead your husband into a close walk with Him and pray for the day when your husband will be willing and able to lead your family spiritually in just the way that best suits his personality and style.

8. Avoid all criticism of your husband in spiritual things; leave it to God to lead him and show him what is right.

Remember that you are the "walking Bible" that your family reads daily. Make sure it rings true because of your devotion and surrender and love for the Lord, and your faithfulness in your personal Bible reading and prayer.

## 46 Q. What should a Christian woman set as her lifetime goals?

**A.** CATHY RICE: Whatever the "lifetime goals" are for a Christian woman, they should be Bible-centered. The Bible has the "how-tos" for all of life—marriage, parenthood, job, talents, etc.

A Christian should always be mindful of the fact that the way we want to go and what we want to do is not always the Lord's way. In Isaiah 55:8 the Lord reminds us, "For my thoughts are not your thoughts, neither are your ways my ways, saith the Lord." With this in mind, a Christian woman should know that her goals in life should be as Proverbs 3:5,6, "Trust in the Lord with all thine heart; and lean not unto thine own understanding. In all thy ways acknowledge him, and he shall direct thy paths."

These are hard verses to follow. I'm afraid, oftentimes, our way seems to make so much more sense than the Lord's way. But, the only way our lifetime goals can be accomplished with satisfaction is to do them God's way.

A. JESSIE: My answer is this:

1. Be a regular, effective witness for the Lord.

2. Develop an always-increasing hunger for Him.

3. Be a consistent influence for good among those whose lives I touch.

4. Help my husband by my love and prayers and my careful attention to home responsibilities.

5. Do everything in my power to help my children be of outstanding character.

6. Have a deep and genuine love for others.

7. Learn to accept myself as God made me; to improve those areas I am able to improve.

8. Enjoy and use the gift of time to the fullest possible measure.

9. Learn how to pray and to spend time in prayer.

10. Be a growing, interesting, always learning, always enthusiastic person.

11. Have a thorough and practical knowledge of the Word of God, make it the moment-by-moment guide in my own life and teach it to others.

12. Seriously consider my gifts and find ways of developing and using them in service for the Lord.

13. Keep a strong sensitivity to sin.

14. Come to the last day of my life with a sense of "completeness" in the Lord Jesus; that there be no sense of futility or wasted purposes to mar my joy and expectation in seeing my Saviour.


# 47 Q. Mrs. Sandberg, how can I be a creative wife?

A. JESSIE: 1. Plan things to do together and with the family that you know your husband would enjoy but won't go to the trouble to plan for himself.

2. If you know he hates to buy gifts, tell him three things you like (size, color, brand specified) and tell him where they can be bought. If he does dare to launch out and buy something on his own, be enthusiastic and thankful about his gift. If the size is wrong and can be exchanged without any "to-do," simply do so without any comment. If you are not happy with the color, you may need to say, "You know, Honey, I've sort of been yearning for a blue sweater to go with that blue plaid skirt I have. I just love the style of the sweater you bought. What do you think of my exchanging it for one of a slightly different shade?" The point is to be careful not to hurt his pride or to make a big deal of insisting on satisfying your own taste always, to the exclusion of his. (Did you know that most husbands who buy clothes for their wives pick out more expensive, better garments than a wife would choose for herself?)

3. Don't always react the predictable way in a given situation. Watch out for comments like, "I *knew* you would say that!" When your husband does something that doesn't turn out right, you may need to learn to say, "I'm sorry that didn't turn out like you hoped it would, Honey. Would it help to talk about it? I'm sure there's a way to work out the problem."

4. Don't use every conversation as an occasion to hammer home some point you've been trying to prove.

5. Listen for clues your husband may be dropping about things he would like to see changed. If he teases you about the way your hair looks at the breakfast table, he may be gently telling you that he would like to see you pay more attention to the way you look. Don't just make excuses for the particular problems he points out; make a mental note that you will keep that problem from coming up again.

6. Interpret correctly the messages he sends you. Ideally, all married couples should verbally express their love for each other. It is also important for everyone to learn to say, "I'm sorry," "I made a mistake," "I feel grouchy," etc. But this has always been easier for women than for men, and there may be times when a wife must read a message of love in act even when it is not spoken in words.

7. While there should never be any question about the position of the husband's authority in the home, there should be occasions when you relieve him of the responsibility of making decisions that you know will not displease him. Sometimes, when my husband would come home late in the evening after some very wearing responsibility, I would ask, "What can I fix you to eat?" I soon learned that he was really too tired to want to plan about food. Many husbands would really rather have a wife "take over" at such a time—to lay out his robe and pajamas, to begin running a hot bath and to have something all ready for him to eat. He might even want all telephone calls intercepted and the children quietly taken care of without his having to handle family matters that would usually be his responsibility. You will know how your husband feels about these things if you take time to notice his reactions under stress.

8. Don't make your husband feel guilty about any sacrifices you must make in helping him: working while he is in school, doing without something so he can start his own business, etc. Make it easy for your husband to grow. (Does he want to go back to school? Does he feel God is calling him into some ministry? Encourage him and back him, even if it means some sacrifice for you. God will make it turn out right!)

9. Make it your responsibility to add lightness and life in the home. Your husband didn't marry you just so he would have someone to wash his clothes and bear his children. He needs you to add color, softness, beauty and joy to his life.

10. Gently and lovingly help your husband to reach his best potential—in the way he looks and dresses, the way he speaks, in his dealings with others. If you resort to nagging, you will do more harm than good.

11. Be single-minded in your attention to his needs. Nothing—absolutely nothing—in the world should come before your being the kind of wife God intended you to be—not your children, your church work or your personal ambitions. Keep your bedroom a quiet, clean and private place—a haven for you two alone. (This is *not* the place to leave laundry waiting to be

folded, or yesterdays newspapers lying around.)

No schedule will work out perfectly, but as far as you are able, plan your late evenings so there will be time for a relaxing bath, a hot cup of tea (or a Coke, if you prefer) together and a few minutes to talk before you go to bed. Many a husband is frustrated by a well-meaning wife who works frantically until bedtime and then falls into bed exhausted and totally unresponsive to her husbands needs.

12. View your marriage as a gift to be cherished and nurtured. HANDLE WITH CARE—polish it gently; protect it from the ravages of wear; enjoy it with gratitude to the God who designed the institution as a beautiful symbol of the relationship between the dear Lord Jesus and His beloved church.

Never forget that you married your husband for what he was— not for what you hoped he would be. Don't consider yourself responsible for "hammering" him into what you think you want in a husband. You will make marks that can never be erased. Love him; enjoy him; find pleasure in his own endearing traits; accept him for what he is. You will find that you have made an investment that will count for eternity.

—From *With Love and a Pinch of Salt,*
Sword of the Lord Publishers.

**48** Q. How can one be friendly while trying to reach her goal in life?

A. MARLENE EVANS: Have you ever decided you were going to be more flexible, let your housework go and give attention to people after hearing a talk on "others" or after watching a "personality kid"? Then, did you soon quit giving that extra attention as your wash piled up, when your house didn't even have a path shoveled through, and when you developed a stress ulcer on top of your tension headache?

Have you ever felt convicted about appearing too busy for visitors at church as you hurriedly said "Hello"? You determined to take time for people and stop running from the Sunday school department to bus route duties to family dinner preparation as if you were a machine! Remember what happened next? Yes, you received the "Miss Friendly" award but you led your Sunday school class into havoc, your bus route into mass confusion, and your family into D.T.'s following Sunday afternoon food withdrawal! Needless to say, you soon gave up really looking at and being friendly toward the very people for whom you were doing the running in your church work. What a dilemma! What is a person to do? Maybe these thoughts will help you.

1. *Always keep in mind that the INDIVIDUAL is your reason for having the larger goal.* Constantly remind yourself that a visitor is your express purpose for being in a growing church. If you teach in a Christian school, tell yourself that you wouldn't have that job were it not for student Susie or Janie or Paul or Harry. (I've often thought how nice I could keep a school room if it weren't for the kids!) And Mother, the son who wants you to watch him put his dog through some new paces is the reason you have your job as homemaker.

2. *Read Bible stories about Jesus and see His care for the individual*—Mary and Martha (Luke 10:38-42); the little children (Matt. 19:13, 14); the washing of feet (John 13:1-17); Lazarus (John 11:1-15); the woman at the well (John 4); and other cases. Studying your Bible from the viewpoint of Jesus' care to and for the individual will keep you in perspective when you feel too busy to give that individual that personal attention.

After Jesus had washed the disciples' feet, He said to them, "If I then, your Lord and Master, have washed your feet; ye also ought to wash one another's feet" (John 13:14).

3. *Pray for wisdom for the balance in keeping a schedule, reaching goals and showing you personally care for people.* God cares that we show our care. He also cares that we do things decently and in order. He is the One who can do the impossible through us if we will let Him!

I heard Mrs. John R. Rice say that she felt we could accomplish more if we would quit fighting. I guess to quit fighting would relax us and allow God to do His work through us.

4. *Practice shifting mental gears.* Sometimes we become frustrated and resentful in being friendly or in showing our friendliness and reaching our goals just because we do not take time to make transitions. So before leaving your car, bus, Sunday school class, home, or office, I suggest you pause a moment for the changing of mental gears. Expect to spend some time speaking to and being friendly to those you meet. Make some small talk when you leave the confines of your personal life. "Use hospitality one to another without grudging," I Peter 4:9 exhorts.

5. *Outline the work you are leaving or the work toward which you are going.* While working at being friendly to people around you in the church parking lot or in the church lobby, you forgot the excellent idea which came to mind for your Sunday school class. Or you were trying to concentrate on what you were talking to a friend about when you were "rudely" interrupted by a phone call.

So why not keep a sketch pad and pencil around—in the office, at school, or in your purse, then sketchily outline the problem you're leaving or the one you are going toward, if you tend to forget them while being friendly to those who might seem to you to be termed "interruptions."

6. *Think of some gracious words that will help you out of situations caused by being friendly.* Friendliness can get you into situations from which you must extricate yourself. For instance, you speak kindly to a little lady—then she begins telling you a one-hour story, or she actually may need your help, yet you must get to your work. Think of some special ways to help you leave graciously, yet at the same time keeping the door ajar. What about: "Oh, I wish I could hear the rest of the story now; perhaps I can later." Or, "I sure want to help you; could I send someone to see you?" Or, "I'm so sorry—I'm already late to my appointment." People need to know you care, that you wish you could stay and talk. "A man hath joy by the answer of his mouth: and a word spoken in due season, how good is it!" (Prov. 15:23).

7. *Saying "Hello" or "Good-by" to a group or to several indi-*

*viduals when you enter or leave is very much appreciated.* Of course, there may be times when you need to slip in or out of a meeting as unobtrusively as possible, and these greetings would not be appropriate, but generally speaking, you and I have found that folks appreciate being acknowledged, even when in a group.

When I was a waitress, I so appreciated customers taking time to look at me and recognize me as some person—something more than a piece of furniture. But some diners didn't know who their waitress was when they needed her.

Transition sentences and changes of atmosphere are as important to smooth relations as having songs to help us through transition times in programs. "A word fitly spoken is like apples of gold in pictures of silver" (Prov. 25:11).

8. *Avoid caring for any business before service time.* You wives of preachers often sit through a service bogged down with a heavy heart because you took care of some W.M.S. business or discussed some person right before the service was to begin. A negative word was given you, but since you didn't have time to figure out the real meaning behind it, you sat there and stewed instead of enjoying the service.

So when someone wants to talk about a school or church problem or an individual—anything that can wait, I suggest you just say, "May I talk to you about it later? I'll call you tomorrow"—in a very friendly manner, of course.

When we do not have time to think through a matter, we can easily get into unnecessary trouble or distress, or forget important information. God wants us to enjoy our Sundays. They are for fellowship, singing, winning souls and praying for each other. "The Lord God hath given me the tongue of the learned, that I should know how to speak a word in season to him that is weary . . ." (Isa. 50:4).

9. *Carry a paper and pen, ready to jot down things you must remember to care for later.* Just a memo can help you remember that phone call or that visit you promised to make, or that letter you promised to write. "He that handleth a matter wisely shall find good . . ." (Prov. 16:20).

113

THERE IS A WAY! No one has to declare "Old Home Week," "Open House," or "Open Office" to prove himself or herself friendly. Balance, moderation and temperance—these are excellent words. You can keep your schedule, reach your God-given goals, yet still show yourself friendly.

Yes, there is a way. Go to Him to find it.

## 49 Q. Is it scriptural for a woman to teach a mixed class of adults?

**A.** JOANNA: The Scripture referred to here is I Timothy 2:11,12: "Let the woman learn in silence with all subjection. But I suffer not a woman to teach, nor to usurp authority over the man, but to be in silence." Kenneth S. Wuest translates these verses:

> Let a woman be learning in silence with every subjection. Moreover, I do not permit a woman to be a teacher [in an official position exercising authority over the man in matters of church doctrine or discipline], neither to exercise authority over a man, but to be in silence, for Adam first was molded, then Eve, and Adam was not deceived, but the woman, having been completely hoodwinked, has fallen into transgression" (*The New Testament: An Expanded Translation*).

This passage seems to teach that women are not to be public teachers in the church, probably because the word teacher carries with it the idea of authority, something women are not given over men in spiritual leadership in the church and home.

The Scripture gives two reasons for this command: 1. Adam was created first, before Eve. 2. Adam was not deceived in the temptation of the serpent, but Eve was; she was completely fooled, deluded, duped.

First Corinthians 11:3 gives God's order: " . . .the head of every man is Christ; and the head of the woman is the man; and the head of Christ is God."

These verses do *not* indicate that women are not to be teachers at all. God used Priscilla and Aquila to explain to Apollos "the way of God more perfectly" (Acts 18:26), but it was evidently done privately, perhaps in their own home. Also, women have the serious and exalted responsibility of teaching children, their own and others, as illustrated by Lois and Eunice, Timothy's grandmother and mother (II Tim. 1:5; 3:15).

## 50 Q. Is a woman to put her Sunday school duty ahead of her family?

**A.** GRACE: I understand your problem, which is very serious in many homes in trying to do the work required of Sunday school teachers.

The work of a Sunday school teacher is very serious and very important, yet there is a growing conviction among spiritual Christian leaders that the church ought to leave more nights open from church activities so good Christians can maintain their home life.

None of us know all the answers. We do know that good Sunday schools are important. A teacher's obligations are very important obligations and a church should have some good standards for teachers. But a woman's duties to her husband and children necessarily must come first in serving the Lord. So you will have to decide what is God's will for you, then do what God shows you is right.

## 51 Q. What if your husband disappoints you?

**A.** FRANCES HOFFMAN: He will—even if he is the grandest husband imaginable. No one can live up to another's expectations all the time. There will be times when he may promise something, fully intending to carry it out; but he may be hindered in fulfilling that promise. Some wives think their husbands can read their minds or should, in some instinctive way, know what they need. But they don't, unless it is discussed in a calm, sweet manner.

Every wife will know the pain of disappointed hopes if she fastens her expectations on her husband. A wise woman will turn her expectations over to God, asking Him to work through her husband. Psalm 62:5 says, "My soul, wait thou only upon God; for my expectation is from him." Only God can fulfill a woman's needs. Only He can make her happy. It is a serious mistake to lay on the husband the heavy burden of always keeping you happy.

If you are deeply grieved and disappointed, you must take the matter to the Lord, asking Him to heal the hurt and give you grace to forgive. Then forgive freely, as Christ forgave you. That is the only thing that will keep you from becoming bitter and hard, and that will keep the marriage together.

A wife should concentrate on doing her part to keep the husband happy and trying not to do anything to disappoint him, rather than on whether he is making her happy or living up to her expectations.

**52** Q. How can I control my tongue? I always end up saying something I wish I hadn't said. I'm also having trouble keeping my thoughts pure. And I have bitter thoughts toward my husband who doesn't live like a Christian, and toward those who have harmed me by saying bad things about me. What do you do about those areas of personal need?

A. JESSIE: When I have said something that I should not have said, in order to get the problem fixed, I make it as bad as it is. I may have to go to a person and say, "What I said really wasn't the truth. I didn't say that quite accurately. It was wrong, and I want you to know that."

In other words, you may need to say, "I'm sorry. I'm a liar!" In the process of saying it, then you make sure you don't get in that pickle again. Or you may have to say, "I was unkind, and I'm sorry."

It is only when we face the wrong use of our tongue and call it what it is, that we really get the grace to get it fixed. We have to face it squarely. Instead, we excuse ourselves. We say, "I always blow off, but I don't really mean it."

A woman said that to me whose husband left her because of her tongue. "He knows I don't really mean those things I say." She had to come to the point of saying, "I did mean it. It was my wicked black heart where those things came from."

The Word of God says it, "Out of the heart the mouth speaketh." When we face that honestly, it helps get it fixed.

**A.** MISS VIOLA: Did you know that one whole chapter in the New Testament is devoted to the tongue? James 3. And hundreds of other verses are given to expose and condemn this most vile, this most sinful, this most evil member in our body.

"My talent is to speak my mind," said a woman to John Wesley. To which he answered, "I am sure, sister, that God wouldn't object if you buried that talent."

Ever hear, "I am not a hypocrite; I say what I think"? or, "I believe in speaking the whole truth and let the chips fall where they may"? Any fool can do those things, says Proverbs 29:11.

We don't get drunk, we don't commit adultery, we don't pull the trigger to commit murder—but the tongue is as deadly as any of these things.

Oh, my constant prayer is, "Set a watch, O Lord, before my mouth and keep the door of my lips . . . ."

**A.** MRS. JOHN R. RICE: There are some very clear verses about how to keep a heart pure, with very specific directions. Philippians 4:8, "Finally, brethren, whatsoever things are true, whatsoever things are honest, whatsoever things are just, whatsoever things are pure, whatsoever things are lovely, whatsoever things are of good report; if there be any virtue, and if there be any praise, think on these things."

The Lord says, "Keep thy heart with all diligence; for out of it are the issues of life" (Prov. 4:23). When these thoughts come, as they will come, use the Scripture. When temptation came to Jesus, He used Scripture: "It is written. . ." (Matt. 4:4,7,10). Don't let filthy thoughts, rebellious thoughts, ugly thoughts, occupy your mind. See that they are cast out. Put right things, beautiful things, sweet things, in their place.

**A.** JESSIE: In other words, you take charge. Don't give your mind over to the Devil's control.

**A.** JOY: On the matter of bitterness, the Scripture specifically says: "Let all bitterness, and wrath, and anger, and clamour, and evil speaking be put away from you, with all malice; And be ye kind, tenderhearted, forgiving one another, even as God for Christ's sake hath forgiven you" (Eph. 5:31,32).

I talked to one girl recently who had a tragic thing done to her by another person. She said, "Do I have to forgive this person? He has never asked my forgiveness. Do I have to forgive him before he asks me?" I used the illustration where Jesus said, "Father, forgive them; for they know not what they do" (Luke 23:24). The Lord Jesus forgave people who did not ask for forgiveness.

When bitterness comes in, as you remember the unfair thing, or what that person did to you that hurt you deeply, I suggest doing as the Scripture says—put away that bitterness.

It might be good to write on a piece of paper, "From this time forth I refuse to think about that again. Lord Jesus, I forgive this person for this hurt," then burn or tear up that paper. Sometimes the physical act of putting it on paper, tearing it up in little pieces and promising the Lord that's out of your mind, is the best antidote. Vow to the Lord that never again will you *mention* the unfairness, even if the memory comes back at times.

**A.** MARY LLOYS: "In the multitude of words there wanteth not sin . . ." (Prov. 10:19). That phrase came back to me over and over again when I was teaching and was talking all day. There are times when we should say nothing. It's not our business to keep everybody else straight; it's not my business to be your conscience. In much talking we are bound to get into sin.

There are times when we have to say, "Lord, help me control my tongue and not say things." Even if I think that person needs to be set right, it is not my business to set her right.

Getting the Scripture in our heart makes it easier to do right. James says if we learn to control the tongue, then we are without sin. I haven't gotten there yet, but I'm working at it!

**A.** GRACE: I think to acknowledge it as sin is the first step, then to choose a Scripture and say, "I won't do it again."

I also think we need to go another step, and that is a little prevention. In what circumstances am I likely to do this? If, for example, I am more likely to talk negatively and critically when I am with some people, then I either need to choose not to be with them, or decide when I'm with them, I'll be positive. I'll not listen to criticism and gossip.

## 53 Q. How does one respond to criticism?

**A.** JOY: First, thank the person for his or her criticism. This is especially true about parents and husbands. "Thank you for caring about me. I'm glad you explained to me how you feel."

Second, if the criticism is valid—for example, if your letters at work really are messy, or if your husband really does frequently have a problem about not having clean socks in his drawer—then the right response is, "I'm sorry. I'm going to do a better job. Here is how I am going to try to improve. . . . Do you have any other suggestions?"

When you respond to constructive criticism with a willingness to be taught, you eliminate the need for argument and it will open the door to the best communication you have ever had. Obviously, if this response is based on your making this choice—"I really want to do right and please the person over me," then God will honor your submission.

If the criticism reveals that you have really offended the person, then be willing to say, "I'm so sorry, Linda. I want you to forgive me for being so irritable with you."

What if you are not sure the criticism is valid? Perhaps in that case you ought to ask another person—your husband or a close friend—to help you look at it objectively. "Is this really the impression that I sometimes give—that I am stuck-up and not interested in people?" Ask the Lord to give you insight, in a prayer something like this: "If the criticism is true, Lord, then please show me and help me fix it. Help me not to be angry at the person just because she told me of my failure."

Even if the criticism seems to have come simply from an attempt to hurt you, remember that God has a lesson for you to learn. Your critics may mean to wound your spirit, but God means it for good. Perhaps He wants you to meet the need of that person. Maybe God wants you to begin to pray for and love your critic, and He is bringing that person to our attention because of his or her great need.

If someone never seems to praise the good things you do but is always quick to point out your failures, remember that a wise man said, "A kick in the pants may send you along further in progress than a pat on the back."

Finally, after you have considered the matter and evaluated what God wants you to do about it, forget the criticism. Sometimes after we are criticized for some little thing, we carry the criticism around all day and feel defeated. To accept the criticism and forget it is a part of learning to "die to self." According to Dr. Lee Roberson, being dead to self simply means being "dead to criticism and dead to praise."

If you plan to serve the Lord fully, then you must decide, "I'm going to do right no matter what people say. If they criticize me unjustly, if they don't seem to notice the special things I do, I'm still going to go right on doing the right thing. I will refuse to let others discourage me by what they say or don't say. I will remember that no matter what the source of criticism, it all comes through the circle of God's love and concern for me, and it can only help me, not hurt me."

# 54 Q. How does one survive the TV football season?

**A.** ELIZABETH: I will share with you how I have survived forty years (or however long they've televised football games) without developing ulcers, going home to Mother, or committing mayhem.

It hasn't been easy. It requires the wiliness of a quarterback, the agility of a place-kicker, and the thick hide of a linebacker. But it can be done.

I'd better tell you, first of all, all the things that *won't* work. It doesn't work to put on a cheerleading uniform and wave a pom-pom in front of the TV so he can't see the game. Tears don't work, at least if you've been married more than a year. He'll just hand you a Kleenex. It won't help to go into the kitchen and bang the pots and pans together, to show how hard you are working. He'll think it's the cymbals in the marching band. Pouting doesn't seem to be effective. (Your mother used to say honey draws more flies than vinegar. Did she tell you why anybody would want to draw flies? Anyway, you'd rather he watch the football game at home than at someone else's house, wouldn't you?)

To be really scientific about this, you maybe ought to find out why you don't like for your husband to watch football.

1. There's something in a woman that just can't stand to see a man sitting down enjoying himself. Don't ask me why; I just know it's true. A woman can think of 1,253 things a man ought

to be doing if he even looks like he is going to sit down and relax. Yes, man works from sun to sun but woman's work is never done. But does that mean he ought never to get to relax? And why couldn't you sit down and relax with him, and go refreshed back to the work that's never done?

2. Football is so, well, brutal, and gory, and male! It just doesn't look very interesting to some women. But God put it in a man's heart to enjoy competition and struggle and physical tests. There's nothing inherently wrong with eleven grown men saying to eleven other men, "We're going to carry this ball over that line; double-dare you to stop us!"

You used to like your husband because he was so masculine. Remember how you used to look up at him when you were first dating and say, "Oh, my, but you're strong"? It wasn't wrong, then, for you to be proud of his strength. It isn't wrong for him to enjoy competitive sports now.

3. "But," you say seriously, and I agree, "it isn't the game; it's the unclad cheerleaders and the beer commercials." These are sometimes offensive, and it's right to be concerned about the impact of the atmosphere of a football game on your family. But a man who loves the Lord can control his television set. He can flip the dial when something undesirable comes on. He doesn't need a mommy to tell him what is suitable for him to watch. He can monitor himself.

Instead of crawling into a corner and sulking during a ball game and spoiling the fun of the whole family, why not cooperate to make it a really happy time?

Your husband will give you some clues about what he'd really like from you. He may want you to sit beside him, analyzing each play like a Howard Cosell. He might be just as happy with your doing something else during a game, and not demanding his attention. You probably ought at least to try to understand the game.

Your husband might enjoy having you sit beside him during a game, even if you knit or crewel instead of following the game closely.

He might want you in the kitchen, dispensing cokes and snacks at frequent intervals. If that's what he seems to want, then do it with such a flare and enthusiasm that the whole family will remember "the day Mom fed Dad."

If the TV set is not portable, and you are planning a meal in front of the set, you may want to use the plastic bags that come with dry cleaning to protect the upholstery and carpet where the small children will be sitting, so you won't have to worry about spills.

For a really important football event (such as the Bowl games on New Year's Day) it might be worth rearranging the living room furniture. Make it so no one has to cross between the TV and the viewers whenever they move.

Some final observations:

When you've worked your fingers to the bone to make it happy for everyone, when you've arranged for all the "togetherness" you can manage, don't expect your husband to be aware of your presence every moment. The purpose of the gathering still is to watch the football game, and that's what he'll be thinking about.

Find out if he wants to answer phone calls during the game, or if he'd like you to take messages for him.

We understand that many good Christians have put away their TV sets because of the ungodly influences of many programs. Other Christians, also sincere and eager to serve the Lord, believe they can enjoy some programs, make them a unique time of family sharing and control the television so it does not harm the family. This is not written to encourage you to watch TV, but rather to help those who are trying to use their TV with discretion, to exercise ingenuity and creativity, to make such a time happy and profitable for the family.

The Apostle Paul said, "One believeth that he may eat all things: another, who is weak, eateth herbs. Let not him that eateth despise him that eateth not; and let not him which eateth not judge him that eateth: for God hath received him. Who art thou that judgest another man's servant? to his own master he standeth or falleth. Yea, he shall be holden up: for God is able to make him stand. . . . Why dost thou judge thy brother? or why dost thou set at nought thy brother? for we shall all stand before the judgment seat of Christ" (Rom. 14:2-10). This is one area, it seems to me, where Christians need to be uncritical and loving of other Christians.

Wouldn't it be funny if it turned out you really *like* football?

—Copyright September, 1981, *The Joyful Woman,*
P. O. Box 90028, Chattanooga, TN 37412,
and used by permission.

# 55 Q. How would you define gossip?

**A.** MARLENE EVANS: I would say that gossip is the giving of bad reports, true or untrue. "A talebearer revealeth secrets: but he that is of a faithful spirit concealeth the matter" (Prov. 11:13).

I would define gossip as idly chattering about the problems of our own family members. Though the chatter may be true, yet we'd be surprised how few would know about it if we didn't tell it. Even if everyone in the world should know it, don't let them hear it from your mouth.

Sometimes we even spread word on ourselves, thus bringing harm to our own name. Example:

Recently I talked to a girl about a suspicion of stealing which was connected with her name. She promptly told friends of the incident. The friends, in turn, told other friends. Later when there was something supposedly taken, some decided it was taken by the girl who had been called into my office.

As far as I know, the girl has never stolen; but I wonder if there won't be an incident happen ten or so years from now, when some thirty-year-old lady will say, "You know, I can't remember all about it, but I think something happened in college connecting her with stealing." It is very possible that this young girl's idle chatter could some day cause her to lose her job.

Often we ourselves are the ones who keep the fire burning; then we wonder how the further word got out! How? We told it! "My heart was hot within me, while I was musing the fire burned: then spake I with my tongue" (Ps. 39:3).

Gossip is revealing our feelings about things we don't like or about something with which we disagree. Why bother giving our little puny opinion when within a few months or years we no longer will hold to that opinion? (We do not refer to Bible doctrines and truths here.)

What is gossip? It is sharing with others those "stupid" things husbands do. Be sure you don't tell the girls anything about your husband that you wouldn't want him to tell the boys about you. By the way, those same girls you talk to think you're pretty stupid for choosing a husband who does such "stupid" things!

After we're over our little miff and hear a girlfriend refer to our husband in a displeasing way, we're ready to fight her, forgetting we're the one who weakened him in front of her.

Gossip is telling your financial status to anyone but God or a godly counselor.

I've been wondering if we who think we know what gossip is and think we don't gossip, really know what gossip is.

Gossip is giving forth bad reports—true or untrue. SO LET'S SHUT UP

. . . about problems (whether widely known or not) in our family or our church;

. . . about our finances;

. . . about things we don't like;

. . . about the stupid things our children, young or grown, do;

. . . about unpleasant things our friends and relatives do;

. . . and, most of all, about the stupid things we ourselves do— unless they happen to be cute little jokes on ourselves.

"But I determined this with myself, that I would not come again to you with heaviness" (II Cor. 2:2). These are all bad reports and can cause nothing but heaviness for us and our listeners. So shut up to people and talk to God!

Let's quit our bad reporting! Let the media do that!

**56** Q. How do you adjust your schedule when your husband is at home and when he is out of town?

A. GERRI HUTSON: When Curtis is away, I have a basic weekly routine that includes home duties, shopping and church functions. I busy myself with reading, sewing, writing letters and having friends in for lunch or dinner.

When my husband is at home, I continue the same routine of home duties, shopping and church functions, but the meals are prepared and served based on his schedule.

I try not to do much entertaining when Curtis is at home. Since he is in front of and with people so much, he needs this quiet time to relax and be with his family.

A. CATHY RICE: My husband was first and foremost in my life. When he came home, I didn't care what happened to the rest of the world. Since he was first, I did what he wanted to do. I loved him. I went with him anywhere he wanted to go. I would let things go to pot, if need be, till he was gone again!


**57** Q. What should you do if there is someone in the church you are jealous of, especially if you are a pastor's wife?

A. CAROLINE ROBERSON: I'm sorry, but I can't help you. I don't have a jealous bone in my body! I have seen miserable wives misinterpret the kindness of the pastor. He has to be all things to all men, and he has to be kind to ladies, too.

I know there are problems. I guess the Lord knew I couldn't handle it, so He didn't let me have a jealous streak. Much of that is in the head anyway. When the imagination starts working, it goes rampant.

Much time on your knees, overlooking a lot of little things, and loving him to death should take care of that.

**58** Q. Mrs. Hyles, please tell us how you keep a house clean with such a busy schedule. Give an example of what you do on separate days.

A. BEVERLY HYLES: I keep my house clean just like you do—with elbow grease! One secret I learned a long, long time ago: before going to bed, go quickly through the house and pick up. It's very discouraging to get up in the morning and find a mess.

I do try to keep a schedule, and I do certain things certain days. I used to be too inflexible. If my schedule got messed up, it threw me for a loop. I'm thankful the Lord has helped me to be more flexible. If somebody needs me, if there's a death, or if I need to visit a sick one and it's my day to wash, I can leave the washing and tend to these matters.

I advise you to make a schedule and stick to it—within reason, of course, except when emergencies arise. A schedule is a great friend in keeping things done.

**59** Q. Dr. Cathy, I sure would like to take off weight, but I don't seem to be able to. Can you help me?

A. CATHY RICE: You might as well decide it's not going to be easy. If it were, there would be no fat people.

In Titus, chapter 2, Paul tells us that we women are to be sober, love our husbands, our children; we are to be discreet, chaste, keepers at home, good, obedient to our own husbands "that the word of God be not blasphemed." One of the guidelines that God gives us is to be "sober." This certainly would refer to wine, but it would also refer to gluttony.

Then I Corinthians 6 tells us that our bodies are the temple of the Holy Ghost, and that we are to glorify God in our bodies. How? Certainly not by gluttony!

Every picture we have in the Bible of a lovely lady is one of a well-kept woman—for example Sarah, at age 60 and 90 was "fair to look upon" (Gen. 12); and the beautiful woman of

Proverbs 31 did not get fat in the midsection, and her arms were not flabby.

Galatians 5:16 tells us "ye shall not fulfill the lust of the flesh." Certainly one of the lusts of the flesh is overeating. In other words, as Philippians 3:19 says, our belly can become our god. And Romans 16:18 says, "For they that are such serve not our Lord Jesus Christ, but their own belly . . . ."

I have heard all the excuses: "Some people are born tall and slim but I am just the short, stout type." Others blame it on heredity—"All of my family are prone to being fat."

I have heard the one, too, about, "Everything I eat goes to fat. Why, I gain on a glass of water." On investigation, however, you usually find there is something more to the water than just water!

But the excuse most frequently heard, and the best excuse for a person being overweight, is, "I have problems with my glands." However, if the truth be known, the real problem is not the *glands* but the *hands.*

Many say to me, "It is easy for you, Mrs. Rice; you are just naturally slim and trim."

No, I am not. I have gone up and down, up and down. Once I gained ten pounds in a short time. I determined to lose those pounds. In reading I came across Proverbs 23:1-3: "When thou sittest to eat . . . consider diligently what is before thee: And put a knife to thy throat, if thou be a [woman] given to appetite . . . ." I told myself I didn't want to be desperate enough to "put a knife to my throat," so I was going to do something about my appetite. I gave myself seven guidelines to help me: I give you those same guidelines hoping they will help you.

1. *Determination.* Don't set goals so high you can't reach them, then become discouraged. Set yourself a goal *and time* to reach it. When you have reached that goal, then set yourself a new one. To help you with your determination, get a verse of Scripture, like Daniel 1:8, "But Daniel purposed in his heart that he would not defile himself with the portion of the king's meat . . . ." I too determined (purposed) not to wreck and ruin my body with fat.

2. *Look often in a full-length mirror;* see all those bumps that need to come off; note the rolls of fat, the flab that needs to go.

(Remember, if you eat rich, fatty foods when no one is looking, the only person you are fooling is yourself.)

3. *Weigh once a week.* Then after reaching your goal, weigh daily. It is so easy to let those extra pounds creep back on.

4. *Have a No-No list.* Avoid bacon, bread, candies, cake, carbonated drinks, popcorn, potatoes, sugars, jellies, macaroni, spaghetti, nuts, pies, pizza. And no seconds. Trim off all visible fat from meats and skim it from soups. Use low-fat or skim milk. Learn to eat slowly. Buy groceries on a full stomach. Buy fresh fruits and vegetables. Leave off junk foods such as potato chips, chocolate candy, nuts, etc. Don't eat between meals. Munch on fruit and vegetables when you get hungry.

5. *Don't eat while standing.* Make yourself sit down everytime you eat. Grabbing a bite here and there, on the run, puts it on!

6. *Go to bed with the rest of the family.* While ironing, cleaning or catching up on our reading, we feel we must eat.

7. *Exercise daily.* We can do a few needed exercises without taking special thought, like walking. Use those two good feet. Walk up and down stairs instead of taking the elevator or escalator. Try to program yourself to walk whenever possible.

And there are three simple exercises you can do while you run your bath.

*Breathe deeply.* If possible, stick your head out a window or door and breathe deeply. Inhale through nose; exhale through mouth twenty times. It makes you feel good, it flushes the body with oxygen and rolls out the excess calories that have been stored in your lungs during the night.

*Stretch to relieve tension.* Find the top of a door or a place where you can reach up and hold tightly. While holding your support, stretch your right leg out as far behind you as you can, at the same time throwing your head backwards. Do this as you count to five, then do the same with your left leg. This helps firm your legs and arms and helps keep the "dowager's bump" off the back of your neck.

*On all fours.* Get down on your hands and knees, then stretch forward as far as you can reach with your chin. Point your nose and chin to the stretching point! Then swing back, sitting down on your heels. As you do this, throw your head backward. This exercise helps to firm your tummy, keep the flab off your arms and it helps the back of your neck.

Now there are exercise machines available, and not too expensive. You might like to price some of them.

How wonderful if one day you can see your children point with pride and hear them say, "That's my mom!" And more than that, to hear your husband say, "There's my wife!"

But don't forget—those pounds can come right back on if you are not careful.


# 60 Q. What is your view of mothers' working today?

A. MRS. JOHN R. RICE: Personally, I wish a woman never had to leave her babies until age six. This is not my idea only, but the idea of educators and scientists as well, that the character of a child is formed in the first six years. These are also the years when their personality is formed. A mother can get a lot of Bible in, in those first six years of a child's life.

Dr. Rice and I prayed with and taught our chidren much. We believed that in those first few years they were trained rather than neglected.

I believe that after children start to school a woman can work, if that must be the case. Personally, I was so wrapped up in my family, taking care of my husband and children and the household, that I could not possibly have had time to work outside our home.

**61** Q. Do you think it is possible for a woman to work outside the home and fulfill her biblical responsibilities to her family?

**A.** JESSIE: Well, obviously I do, or I wouldn't have taught at Tennessee Temple College while rearing my family!

A working wife/mother needs to look often at the beautiful example of the great working lady of Proverbs 31. She ran her home so successfully that the Scripture says of her, "Her children arise up, and call her blessed; her husband also, and he praiseth her." Aside from her responsibilities of providing a bountiful table for her family and servants, making beautiful warm clothing for her family, shopping carefully, and keeping her home in order, she also bought real estate, made and sold fine linen girdles and took care of the needs of the poor in her neighborhood.

The secret is that she kept her priorities straight, she worked terribly hard, and she earnestly sought to please the Lord. We know that making her husband happy and successful was her first priority because the Bible says of her, "The heart of her husband doth safely trust in her, so that he shall have no need of spoil. She will do him good and not evil all the days of her life." While she may have found personal fulfillment in the many jobs she did, her family's interests were her first concern. There was never a question of her neglecting her home or her responsibility to the Lord in order to find personal satisfaction.

Let me add a personal note here. My own preference for my life has been to be a non-working mother. I like cooking and keeping house, but in the process of working out of necessity, outside the home, God has given me a wider opportunity for blessing others.

**A.** JOY: Yes, I believe a woman can work outside the home and be a successful homemaker under certain conditions: First, that she has the full support and approval of her husband; second, that she has the physical and emotional stamina for a very demanding life; third, that she has a specific, worthwhile purpose to fulfill in her working; fourth, that she has assurance that her children are being well cared for in her absence; and finally, that she be confident that she is in the center of God's will.

I think it is generally better for a woman to be in the home a major part of the day, especially if she has small children not in school. But today some Christian families are choosing for the mother to work at least part-time so the children can attend a Christian school.

**A.** GRACE: Let me add to this several thoughts since this is an important decision that cannot be taken lightly.

This question is frequently of importance in Christian families for several reasons. Many pastors and Christian workers serve the Lord at lower wages than they might be able to get at other jobs. This often leaves a gap between the income and the actual needs of the family. As Joy mentioned, Christian families often feel, and rightly, that their children must be in a Christian school, and this is so important it is worth sacrifices. Yet it is easy to choose one good thing over another that is better, and there is a real conflict in making the choice as to whether the wife will work.

Some guidelines may be helpful in considering this choice:

1. The Bible command for a wife to be submissive to her husband must be in operation here. The decision must be made jointly if a Christian wife is to work.

2. The wife is still responsible for the housework, even though she is working. Most husbands are willing to share the load, but in this case the wife must request, not demand, his help.

3. A working wife must beware of the tendency to think and speak of "my money" and to plan to use it however she alone decides. He shares in the decision, if she is an obedient wife.

4. Even secular authorities warn about the danger of using the wife's income to elevate the lifestyle. It is so easy to buy little luxuries and to continually improve the home that a working wife may find she is working long after there is a need, simply because she wants to buy more and nicer things.

5. The most obvious danger in a Christian wife's working is her relationship with men. Even the most devoted wife needs to guard against an improper attitude toward the men she works with. In a worldly situation, there will be innuendoes and compliments and suggestive stories, and many times a Christian wife, before she knows it, is caught up in something shameful and even tragic. No woman should trust herself in this area; she must constantly be on guard to avoid leaving the wrong impression or letting herself become very friendly with any man—even a good man—she works with.

Many Christian women do work, and serve God, and stay faithful to their husbands and lovingly meet their children's needs. It is a difficult task and a tiring one, and requires constant grace and help from the Lord. She will need to pray more, read the Bible more, and be more sensitive to her husband's wishes than if she didn't work.

**62** Q. Mrs. Martin, do you ever have conflicts about home and work? Do you ever feel guilty about not being at home more?

A. JOY: I told you that I did resign from being a mother twice last week, only Roger wouldn't accept my resignation! I frequently feel a conflict, then I have to go to my husband and say, "What do I do?"

I want to mention one thing that's very important. Several people have asked me, "How do you do this, and do this, and do this?"

I can honestly tell you that everything on my schedule is something my husband not only approved but in most cases, pushed me into! I don't accept speaking engagements without asking him. I have to have confidence that I'm doing what pleases him. I talked to him on the phone today, just before I got ready to speak. I needed that reassurance—"I'm praying for you, Honey, and we love you." He gave me good words about the children.

For example, I was gone last night. That meant Daddy did some special things with the family. Last night Daddy took Marilou, our fifteen-year-old, out for a special dinner. I don't need to feel guilty, because I know he is doing some special things that he needs to do himself for our children.

If God calls you to do a particular thing, it may be very difficult. There are lots of times I cry and say, "I'd love to stay home and bake bread." (I've never baked bread in my whole life! One of these days I'm going to!) Right now I'm just trying to do what the Lord tells me to do, and what my husband tells me to do.

Just believe that if God calls you to do something, He will give you the strength to do it, and a husband to back you in it.

## 63 Q. How do you justify traveling or working when you make such a big point of being a wife and mother?

**A.** JESSIE: It is really what Joy made reference to. She was teasing me on the plane, "Jessie, have you finally accepted the fact that God has called you to be a teacher?"

My husband is the one who wanted me to teach. I like homemaking best. I did bake bread, Joy! I would love to be at home. I used to ask, "Honey, why do I have to teach?" At first I thought it was because we needed the money to put our children through a Christian school. Finally my husband said, "Why don't you just face the fact that God has a ministry for you?" Finally, after all these years, I'm learning that God does have a ministry for me.

Sometimes the Lord does give you an opportunity to do something outside the home, but it can only be done in relationship to what your husband wants. You must have his blessing or the Lord won't honor it.

**64** **Q. Do you work outside the home? If so, how do you handle it?**

**A.** CAROLINE ROBERSON: I am home about all the time. I am a housewife. I don't want to teach or do any other work outside the home. It's not that I'm not mentally capable! I just push my husband. I stay behind him.

When my boy was two years old I was asked to supply in the business department, so I taught typing. It was supposed to be just for a few weeks but I ended up doing it a year and a half. I said, "Lord, that's for the birds. I don't like to teach." It has to be a real calling to be a teacher. So I'm a proud housewife. I do travel a good deal with my husband to attend to his needs, but I have only home responsibilities.

**65** **Q. How can a mother learn to cope with the pressures of daily caring for children when there are few opportunities for "getting away"?**

**A.** JESSIE: I found I had to constantly be reminding myself that I was busy developing future "kings and priests" (Prov. 23:24, 25) and that was a great encouragement to me. I also had to learn to put certain personal goals "on hold" while my children were young, reminding myself that someday there would be time for other projects. Even though I rarely had large blocks of time for getting away from my responsibilities, I did try to put small cushions in the schedule, like having my own private "tea party" while the children were sleeping, or saving a half hour every afternoon for reading in a favorite book.

**66** **Q. Have you any suggestions about creating a good home atmosphere in living in rented homes, or parsonages where one cannot make major changes?**

**A.** MARY LLOYS: Since I have moved many times, we have had opportunities galore to live happily in lovely new parsonages, primitive rented homes, and owning our own home three times—the longest time for seven years.

We have made a point of routinely carrying an unreasonable number of keepsakes: family portraits, oil paintings, treasured old pieces of furniture, even old stuffed toys, the children's cribmates. We nearly always have planted a peace rose in the yard, and I have a particular liking for hyacinths, so I like to plant bulbs that scent the air with that heady perfume. We try to make each home our own, something for all of us to enjoy.

There is a whole row of pine trees planted along a property line in Millington, Tennessee, that my husband planted. The tallest one marks the grave of Pug, our beloved mongrel dog who brightened our lives for twelve years.

In nearly every house we have painted the living room wall a colonial blue, and our master bedroom the same peaceful shade. We still treasure the oak table and buffet that were given us thirty years ago by missionary friends, and the mahogany lowboy we received in the same fashion. A little oak desk, given our children by a favorite third-grade teacher, now graces our dining room—it has graduated from children's bedrooms.

We still carry the same carrom board, pizza pan, ping-pong set, and most of the same books and records that the older children enjoyed as youngsters. Our grandchildren now can read what Daddy or Mommy enjoyed as a child. We have been happy nearly all the time, content in knowing we are in God's place for us.

## 67 Q. Should a pastor's wife be the head of church groups or organizations, or should she let others do it?

A. BEVERLY HYLES: Your question struck a note with me, because many wonder how much a pastor's wife should do. Should she take the leadership of different groups, and so forth? Of course, this depends upon: what her husband wants her to do, what she is qualified to do, what she feels the Lord wants her to do, and how old her children are. Many things are involved.

When our children were small, my husband wanted me to teach and serve the Lord, but he preferred I not take any big responsibilities, such as being President of the Women's Missionary Society. He preferred me to be in the background—just keeping the home fires burning, so to speak.

Now some pastors would prefer their wives to be more active. But it boils down to what does your husband want. Ask his advice, then do what he would like you to do in the service for Christ.

**68** Q. Mrs. Sandberg, I've got problems and more problems. How can I handle them all?

A. JESSIE: There is one element of life which we do all share whether we are young or old, rich or poor, educated or uneducated, married or single. We all have problems! Even the child of God, because he is still living in a frail human body and is operating with a fallen nature in a world corrupted and contaminated by sin, has problems.

The difficulties of life, in themselves, are not necessarily bad. It is our method of handling problems that brings either success or failure. This is what God says about getting answers to problems:

1. Be totally submissive to the will of God. When a problem seems unsolvable, it is often because somewhere along the road we have stepped out of God's will and have started down a path of our own choosing. God cannot reveal His direction for us until we turn our backs on our own stubborn way. Very often the answers come to us clearly and simply when we come to the point where we can say: "Lord, I am Your property and You have a right to do with me whatever You choose. I submit myself to Your will."

When you come to the place of wanting God's will in your life more than any other thing, you will see your problems in a new perspective, and see solutions you have not recognized before. "He that findeth his life shall lose it; and he that loseth his life for my sake shall find it" (Matt. 10:39).

2. Search the Word of God for answers to your particular problem. Recognize that God knew your special difficulty long before it arose and He has prepared answers in His Word that will help you find solutions. Search for the answers just as diligently as you would search for a valuable piece of lost jewelry. As you rest on the Word of God, you will find you are not nearly so upset by some of the situations that have caused you annoyance and grief. The very act of reading and meditating on the Word will make the problems less troublesome. "Great peace have they which love thy law, and nothing shall offend them" (Ps. 119:165).

3. Humbly and faithfully meet with God in the closet of prayer for answers to your problem. Give God a chance to prove that He can do what He has promised to do.

—From her book, *With Love. . . and a Pinch of Salt,*
Sword of the Lord Publishers.

**69** **Q. What is it that takes one away from the Word of God?**

**A.** MARLENE EVANS: The answer is—everything. The world, the flesh and the Devil see to that!

Anyone knows that all the extra activity of a Daily Vacation Bible School, a week of revival, a lovely holiday, or a great family vacation can keep us running until we're too fagged out to pick up the Bible, let alone read, study and meditate on the Scripture. Yes, a very good thing can keep us from the Bible as quickly as a very bad thing can.

You'd think the death of a loved one would drive us to the Bible; however, sometimes we rely on the comfort of people more than on God at that crucial time. Haven't you found it so?

It seems sickness would cause us to run to the Bible; however, I'm afraid that even in times of sickness we may sometimes feel too apathetic to pick up the blessed Book. Isn't that right?

Here's a list of things which can keep us away from the Word of God, our spiritual life-support system. So beware!

| | |
|---|---|
| 1. Vacations | 18. Sickness |
| 2. Houses | 19. Television |
| 3. Possessions | 20. Nature |
| 4. Pleasures | 21. Sports |
| 5. Friends | 22. Hobbies |
| 6. Jobs | 23. Death of loved one |
| 7. Church work | 24. Excessive grooming |
| 8. Marriage | 25. Excessive shopping |
| 9. Wedding | 26. Dating |
| 10. Music | 27. Work around the house |
| 11. Books, newspapers | 28. Daily Vacation Bible School |
| 12. Holidays | 29. Bible conference |
| 13. Magazines | 30. Camp |
| 14. Revivals | 31. Excessive doing for others |
| 15. Children | 32. Financial worries |
| 16. Soul winning | 33. Fear of appearing pious |
| 17. Family reunions | 34. Overt sin |

What else can you add to this list? What excuse do you use?

Now don't think I'm against family reunions, for example. The truth is, I am an avid believer in family ties. Don't think I'm giving you Bible readers who are non-soul winners a pat on the back. If you're in the Bible in a right way, you'll go soul winning! I am just asking, How do your excuses justify you for not loving and not reading the Bible?

## 70 Q. I want to be sold out for Christ, lose my life every day. How do I do that?

A. JESSIE: When I was a teenager I once came across Matthew 10:39 in my daily devotional reading and I remember puzzling for a long time over its meaning: "He that findeth his life shall lose it; and he that loseth his life for my sake, shall find it."

I had often heard missionaries quote the verse and I assumed that it referred entirely to one's physical life. Obviously, a martyr who gave his life for the cause of Christ would have some special reward in Heaven; and by the same token, any Christian who refused to stand true to Christ in a time of great persecution was only wasting his life even though he saved it.

It was only after I became a grown woman that I began to understand that losing one's life for Christ's sake might have implications for Christians in the everyday routines of life—rearing children, keeping a home, working at a job, buying groceries, visiting with friends, teaching a Sunday school class—and so on.

Sometime ago I made a list of those things which the Lord might require of me *today*. To lose myself for the cause of Christ may mean:

1. To be willing to give up my privacy. Almost every kind of spiritual ministry requires involvement with people.

2. To be willing to accept a thousand little impositions on my schedule—taking time for telephone calls, little notes of encouragement, visits to the unsaved, the ill, the bereaved—even when I have many other responsibilities.

3. To deny myself the satisfaction of being disgusted with people who are spoiled and backslidden and critical; to learn to love anyway.

4. To be willing to give cheerfully the things which other people require of me as a wife, a mother, a Sunday school teacher, a neighbor.

5. To squelch a natural tendency to nurse along my own hurts, and dwell on my own discomforts.

6. To refuse to allow myself to constantly analyze and hash over my own weaknesses and imperfections and, instead, to turn them over to the Lord.

7. To practice a life of faith even when I do not "feel" a deep faith. To make decisions and fulfill responsibilities not on the basis of what I can see, but on what God has promised.

8. To keep doing the job God has given, even in the face of opposition, ridicule, disappointment and seeming failure.

9. To seek the power of the Holy Spirit in my life even when I know that the fulness of the Holy Spirit may mean giving up some of the things which I have hitherto felt to be of top importance to me.

10.  To be willing to be misunderstood, slighted, maligned and taken for granted in doing the work God has given me to do.

I hope these will help you to "lose" yourself.

# P.S.

*Some additional help by Christian leaders: a doctor, spiritual counselors, a psychologist, and others who have influenced America and the home.*

# Education of our Children

## DR. L. E. MAXWELL

There is a great battle today about Christian education. And this conflict centers around who owns the child, the parents or the state. To whom does the child belong? That is the question. Unless we come to a well-defined conclusion on this point, we cannot proceed safely with the subject of his education. To be undecided on the question of who owns the child is to be undecided all along the line, and we shall lose the battle.

Who owns the child? The answer to this question affects the whole destiny of the child—for both time and eternity. It goes into the whole manner of dealing with him, his friendships, his education, what he shall learn and not learn. The conclusion we reach will determine our aims and aspirations respecting his future, his calling and lifework, even his very eating and drinking and daily behavior.

To whom does my child belong? Does he belong to this world? to some selfish ambition? to the state? to myself? or to God? For whom am I to teach and train him? Today's welfare world and the socialized state are making inroads on the family and are presuming to determine the direction and education and thinking of our young ones—brainwashing them!

Christian parents would say in theory, "Our children belong to God," but very often the parents' conduct and practice belie their words. We must waken afresh to the fact that our children are a sacred trust, a stewardship, and a God-given inheritance. Others, such as friends and pastors and teachers, will of course have some part in influencing our children; but we as parents are, above all others, responsible for what our young "Timothy" or our little "Samuel" will become. We are to train up each child "in the way he should go."

Some people hold the strange view that children should not be influenced toward Christianity, but left without religious training. We, therefore, have schools that are plainly infidelic, where the story of God's love, as shown in the life and death of His Son, is studiously avoided. Yes, we have even Protestant schools where the Bible is almost entirely omitted. The argument is that children should be left unbiased until they reach years of discretion.

The poet Coleridge once wrote, "I have a friend who holds these views, and I asked him to come and admire my garden."

"How can I?" he replied, "for I see that it is all overgrown with weeds."

"That," I answered, "is because it has not yet come to years of discretion, and I did not think it right to prejudice it in favor of strawberries and roses."

We must not forget the distinct track of the educational training—*the way in which the child should go.* The more early the training, the more easy the work, and the more encouraging the results. Our character largely takes the form of that mold into which our early years were cast. Much in afterlife, both good and evil, may be traced back to the seeds sown in our earliest days. It is a simple matter of experience that what is early learned is most firmly retained. We should therefore take advantage of the pliability of youth, just as the gardener begins to graft at the first rising of the sap in the spring.

In the matter of educating our children, we can begin our work too late, but we can scarcely begin it too soon. If our children are too young to teach to read, they cannot be too young to teach to obey. And obedience is one of the first lessons of true education.

The Christian conception of education is laid down in Deuteronomy 6:4-9. Here is a system of parental instruction so ordered as to carry godly principles into daily life and have them perpetuated to coming unborn generations.

Solomon gives a word of warning regarding false education when he says: "Cease, my son, to hear the instruction that causeth to err from the words of knowledge" (Prov. 19:27). Martin Luther spoke the truth when he said, "I am much afraid the universities will prove to be the great gates to Hell, unless they diligently labor to explain the Holy Scriptures and to engrave them upon the hearts of youth. I advise no one to place his child where the Scriptures do not reign paramount. Every institution where men are not unceasingly occupied with the Word of God must become corrupt."

# The Ideal of Womanhood

MYRNIA F. FARNHAM, M.D.

A clear majority of all adult American women are engulfed today in emotional difficulties. They come to me complaining about their "nerves," and generally confide that they feel everlastingly ill at ease, empty, out of step with the world, unhappy, neurotic. And the more they are involved in careers, the more they are childless, the more they are fashionably dressed and elaborately made up, the longer is the list of their troubles.

A larger proportion of the patients who consult me about emotional disorders are the feminine careerists, women who have invaded the "big league" of male competition and have held their own successfully. Behind their chic facades, they are usually a sorry sight—a bundle of nerves, frustrations and anxieties. If they have married at all, typically they have at least one divorce behind them.

Then there are the women who have no careers—but wish they had. Apologetically they explain to me that they are "just housewives." They lament the "boredom" and "drudgery" of their lives; they fiercely resent the fact that they are women. To occupy themselves, they gamble away their husband's money at bridge, at the wheel, fritter it in aimless shopping, or listen (watch) hour after hour to silly soap operas.

Today, the typical home is becoming an empty shell. People rarely stay home to have their "fun." There are now a multitude of outside diversions: movies, dance halls, taverns, nightclubs, bowling alleys, golf courses. The home, an efficient yet dreary hole-in-the-wall, has morning and evening rush hours, but during most of the day it is either vacant or practically so.

There is one type of woman rarely seen in a psychiatrist's office. That is the woman who is glad she is a woman. Although now a minority in our female population, she honestly enjoys homemaking and, more than anything in the world, wants to raise a family of healthy, normal youngsters. During twenty years of listening to distressed patients, I have never met her in my office—because she doesn't need help.

Acclaim goes to the woman who acquires two college degrees, becomes a foreign correspondent, emerges from three marriages as from train wrecks, brings one neurotic brat into the world, and sounds off regularly on current affairs, just like a man.

Despite such propaganda, the fact is that a woman who succeeds in rearing several normal, well-adjusted youngsters to maturity is actually accomplishing a feat of much greater difficulty, intricacy and importance than most men accomplish in their lifetimes. No one thinks to give such a woman credit if one son becomes a judge, another a great engineer, a third a scientist. Yet certainly such an achievement requires vastly more skill and ingenuity than being a high-powered female sales-executive.

It is time we recognize motherhood as our most vital—and one of our most highly skilled—professions, and exalt it as such.

# Working Mother vs. Homemaker

TIM and BEVERLY LaHAYE

**Q.** *Could you give me some spiritual guidance and Scripture concerning the importance of a young mother's being at home with her small children, rather than her working outside the home?*

**A.** Today we hear a lot about working mothers. We see material written to help working mothers to be more effective while at home. So we begin to go along with the tide and think, Well, why not? Everybody else is doing it. But I think it is good to stop and ask oneself, Should I be working? Is it really right in God's eyes?

It is very difficult to give a pat answer because within each home there are different circumstances needing different solutions. So let's start with the main point to this question: Should a young mother be working? We have to consider her priorities.

What are the priorities of any mother?

Well, her first priority is to God. She is to be a godly woman, to develop herself spiritually, to be in the Word, to grow in grace and knowledge of the Lord Jesus Christ and to put God first in everything she does.

Her second priority would be to her husband. She married him before there were children. So, after God, she is under the authority of her husband—the head of her home.

Her third priority would be to her children.

Little children come into the home not asking to come. They come as helpless little creatures who depend on Mother and Dad for their very life. It is in the child's early years that he will develop faster physically, mentally and in every other way than at any future time of his life.

One-half of the intellectual capacity of an adult has already been developed by the age of four. This is not his knowledge, but his capacity for taking in knowledge. Eighty percent is developed by the age of eight. This is quite a startling statistic when one realizes that the time a mother spends with him during his first four years will determine the quality of that 50 percent of his total intellectual capacity.

It is very important that a small child, during those years, be in the company of someone who is going to instill within him good principles, values and a philosophy that will produce good character.

This same idea of influencing the first four years of children is behind the International Year of the Child. There is the obsession on the part of so many individuals in our government to get children into preschool or day-care centers. They want to control the minds of our children.

I read about an educational expert with the Department of Health, Education and Welfare who stated that educators have learned through the public school system (at the cost of billions of taxpayers' dollars) that they cannot undo in 13 years of education the "harm" done to children prior to their starting school. He did not have in mind the child who is abused or neglected and so on—he had religious children in mind. He was talking about children who are coming to school with preconceived convictions, concepts, priorities and moral values.

They want children to come to school almost like automatons with their "unfettered" brains in neutral. They know what we know and what God knew—that the most influential person in the first few years of a child's life is his mother. Next to mother in influence is the father. This is why God gave children the home. If parents prepare their children properly before they go to school, they will find that their children will have a lifetime of guidelines and principles to operate by.

The National Education Association (NEA) has already gone on record stating that they are in favor of reducing the required attendance age for school children to two years. That will give them an additional 8,000 hours of a young child's life to form him, train him and lead him in the views which would cause him to go in the direction *they* choose.

The tragedy is that many selfish parents and those who are interested in material possessions think, "Oh, that is great! Let the public school take care of my children. Then I can go to work." Well, it may solve a few temporary economic problems, but it is going to create havoc later on.

Do you know where this whole concept comes from? It comes right out of Moscow. We saw it. We were there. We saw the school children. We saw how brainwashed they were against their parents. Parents in communist countries are betrayed by their own children because the preschool/day-care centers are run by hard-core communists who teach that the State and the Communist Party are more important than Mother and Father. Therefore, when they get into the first, second and third grade and see their parents do something traditional for old Russia, they can go to the communist leaders to turn them in.

The humanists cannot seem to corrupt our kids fast enough with a college, high school, junior high and elementary education, so they want to corrupt them in preschool and day-care centers.

I am certain that a young mother, if at all possible, should be at home with her small children during those early years before they go to school. I realize that, in some instances, this is impossible. Examples might include a young wife whose husband is going to school or whose husband has died, or a divorce situation in which the mother is forced to work just to keep food on the table. To these individuals I would say that very special care should be taken in the selection of a baby sitter. Be certain that the sitter will continue to instill within the child the same ideals that you have in your home. She or he should teach the child the same philosophy and values that will reinforce what you are trying to accomplish in your home.

Under normal circumstances, God gave six adults to each child—four grandparents and two parents. Thus, if for some reason the parents cannot fulfill their full-time role, then Christian grandparents should be the first consideration as guardians, provided they maintain the same standards. Otherwise it should be someone who shares your Christian principles and philosophies of life.

God has given you the privilege and responsibility of raising and training your child. You should never want this privilege to be put in the hands of the government or of another organization, which may not train your child in the way in which God has instructed.

What you must understand is that the government recruits their employees out of secular colleges. These colleges embrace humanistic, atheistic and evolutionary philosophies that are in total opposition to the Christian persuasion.

I would encourage you to read Proverbs 31. I am sure you have probably read it before, but take a long look at this dear woman and notice that all of her activity is centered around her family. All of her shopping, business projects and meetings in the market place are centered around what she is doing to help develop and benefit her family.

A young mother can learn much from this. She should not be concerned with developing her own individuality in an outside career, but rather in developing it through building up her own family. Proverbs 22:6 says, "Train up a child in the way he should go: and when he is old, he will not depart from it." In doing this she can then say, "I have no greater joy than to hear that my children walk in truth" (III John 4).

—From *Good News Broadcaster*

# A Christian Wife's Deportment

## GEORGE MUELLER

The late George Mueller, founder of the wonderful Christian orphanages of Bristol, England, relates the following story which we feel will be a real encouragement to Christian wives with unbelieving husbands; and at the same time is a beautiful illustration of I Peter 3:1, 2.

There lived at Basle an opulent citizen whose wife was a believer, but he himself feared not the Lord. His practice was to spend his evenings in a wine-house, where he would often tarry till eleven, twelve, or even one o'clock. On such occasions his wife used to receive him most kindly, never reproach him in the least, either at the time or afterwards, nor complain at all on account of his late hours, by which she was kept from seasonable rest. Moreover, if it should be needful to assist him in undressing himself when he had drunk to excess, she would do this also in a very kind and meek way. Thus it went on for a long time.

One evening this gentleman was again, as usual, in a wine-house, and having tarried there with his merry companions till midnight, he said to them: "I bet if we go to my house, we shall find my wife sitting up and waiting for me. She herself will come to the door and receive us very kindly. If I ask her to prepare us a supper, she will do it at once, without the least murmur or unkind expression or look."

His companions in sin did not believe his statement. At last, however, after some more conversation about the strange statement (as it appeared to them), it was agreed that they would all go to see this kind of wife. Accordingly they went. After they had knocked, they found the door immediately opened by the lady herself. They were all courteously and kindly received by her.

The party having entered, the master of the house asked his wife to prepare supper for them, which she, in the meekest way, at once agreed to do. After awhile, supper was served by herself without the least sign of dissatisfaction, or murmur, or complaint.

Having now prepared all for the company, she retired to her room. When she had left the party, one of the gentlemen said, "What a wicked and cruel man you are to thus torment so kind a wife!" He then took his hat and stick, and without touching a morsel of the supper, went away. Another made a similar remark and left without touching the supper. Thus one and another left till they were all gone without tasting the supper.

The master of the house was not left alone, and the Spirit of God brought before him all his dreadful wickedness, especially his great sins toward his wife. The party had not left the house half an hour before he went to his wife's room, requesting her to pray for him, saying he felt himself a great sinner and asking her forgiveness for all his behavior toward her. From that time on he became a disciple of the Lord Jesus.

Observe:

(1) The wife acted in accordance with I Peter 3:1. She kept her place as being in subjection and the Lord owned it.

(2) She reproached not her husband, but meekly and kindly served him when he used to come home.

(3) She did not allow the servants to sit up for their master, but sat up herself, thus honoring him as her head and superior, and concealed also, as far as she was able, her husband's shame from the servants.

(4) In all probability, a part of those hours, during which she had to sit up, was spent in prayer for her husband, or in reading the Word of God, to gather fresh strength for all the trials connected with her position.

(5) Be not discouraged if you have to suffer from unconverted

relatives. Perhaps very shortly the Lord may give you the desire of your heart, and answer your prayer for them; but in the meantime seek to commend the truth, not by reproaching them on account of their behavior toward you, but by manifesting toward them the meekness, gentleness, and kindness of the Lord Jesus Christ.

*"Likewise, ye wives, be in subjection to your own husbands; that, if any obey not the word, they also may without the word be won by the conversation of the wives; While they behold your chaste conversation coupled with fear."*—I Pet. 3:1,2.

# How Much Should a Child Be Told?

## DR. CLYDE NARRAMORE

(Author of many books in the field of psychology, child training,youth guidance and pastoral counseling.)

**Q.** *It seems that today our children read so much in the various magazines, as well as hearing the subject of sex discussed at school, that we parents are the last to give them the facts. Just how much should children be told?*

**A.** You have heard the old saying, "Things are seldom what they seem." In a sense, questions about sex are not always what *they* seem. For example, when little Johnny asked his parents where he came from, he did not have the slightest thought about sex. He had heard the other children tell which state they were born in and he merely wanted to get his own birthplace straight. "Was it Kansas or Missouri?"

It is possible to tell your child too much about sex—more than he really wants to know. This is why *listening* is as important as explaining.

Listen carefully to what your child asks. Fortunately he does not want or need a lengthy, technical lecture. Furthermore, a simple, honest answer is more easily understood.

You can easily tell when a youngster's curiosity is satisfied. If there are no more questions—if he starts looking for his baseball—or if he asks for a peanut butter sandwich, you can be sure he has all of the information he wants or needs just now.

It has been said that an adult can talk about sex for hours, but a small child's interest usually lasts for about thirty seconds! Too much information is bewildering and confusing. It can also stimulate a child's interest too early.

The amount you tell a child depends partly upon his age. Very young children do not understand much about causes, results and implications. For example, a child of three may ask, "Where do babies come from?"

You might answer, "They grow inside the mother until they are big enough to live in the outside world." To a child approximately four or five years old you might add, "All children come from their parents—from their mother and daddy. Each baby starts as a tiny little baby inside the mother. Then it grows and grows until it is big enough to live outside the mother."

As a child grows older he will ask more about the same questions. Some parents make the mistake of reading their own adult understanding into the child's question. But to go too deeply into this is neither wise nor necessary.

# Our Children's Questions

### ORD L. MORROW

We are born with questions in our very souls, and that is as it should be. The first four words a child generally learns are: "mama," "papa," "no" and "why." The wise parent does all he can to keep alive that yearning to know. We should never allow ourselves to grow impatient at a child's "why?"

As the child grows his questions will become increasingly difficult to answer. He may start with, "Why doesn't the sun fall out of the sky?" then go on to the much more profound "Why doesn't God show His face in the heavens?" and "Why doesn't He speak in an audible voice so we can hear Him?"

The child will echo a thousand questions which you yourself had in your heart at some time. Other questions include: "Can God be reached by prayer?" "Is He a God who knows what is going on in my little corner of the universe?" "Does He care when things get tangled up and go wrong for me?" "Does He care when my heart is hurt, when my life is rushed, hectic and burdensome?" "Does He have a word for me when my mind is dark and my heart is confused?" "Can He do anything about the things I have done which make me hate myself?" "Does He have compassion?" "Can He forgive? and will He?" "Can He speak peace to the wretched, the miserable and the ashamed?"

The pity is that many of the questions of our children must go unanswered. We are embarrassed because we cannot answer them, so we hush them up and hurry them out to play with their questions still unanswered. When they grow up we send them off to school or off into the big world with their questions still unanswered—and that can be a tragedy. We ought to be very

159

ashamed and sad that we cannot answer the questions which are asked by honest and serious sons and daughters.

One reason why we have so few satisfying answers may be that in recent years we have had a tendency to worship man rather than God. We call this humanism. Humanism says that man is the measure of all things. So, glory to man in the highest! It matters not if the approach is from an optimistic or a pessimistic view of man—we still cannot answer those searching and honest questions. Such failure ought to humble us, haunt us, hurt us and awaken us.

We thought we could work out our own salvation, structure our own scheme of values and make science and education and our power to think ends in themselves. But something has gone wrong. We are no nearer to honest answers than we ever were. We tried to explain away the supernatural, and found that we had nothing to put in its place. We have exalted the creature more than the Creator until the sun is nothing but a ball of fire and the stars are nothing but little twinkling points of light. The Scriptures say, "The heavens declare the glory of God" (Ps. 19:1), but we said, "Not so; they say nothing at all." We have substituted self-expression for the will of God, and the rule of man for the rule of God. But we still have not answered the simple questions of our children.

It does seem that we should not lay too much claim to wisdom before we can give honest, adequate answers to our questioning children. We ought to quit acting so high and mighty until we can answer the questions concerning sin, the thing that causes us to blow out the light of God and beat up our brothers. And we should walk softly until we can answer the questions concerning hope, peace and death. Our world is sinning and dying, and we dare not even mention it. What a heritage to leave our children! They ask simple, honest and sincere questions; we look at them blankly and say nothing.

—From *Good News Broadcaster*

# "Spocked," or Spanked?

DR. L. E. MAXWELL

Long president of Prairie Bible Institute and
Editor of *Prairie Overcomer*

Dr. Benjamin Spock, author of the once-famous book, *Baby and Child Care*, finally admitted that if today's children are "brattier" than those of a former generation, he must share part of the blame. His present claim: "Inability to be firm is, to my mind, the commonest problem of parents in America today." He terms today's impudent, unruly children as "brattier," and places the blame, in part at least, on the self-appointed experts— "the child psychiatrists, psychologists, teachers, social workers, and pediatricians like myself."

It was indeed the philosophy of Spock and those of his sort that spawned the present generation of permissive-minded parents. And such parents have in turn begotten and brought up a brood of disagreeable and discontented young rebels. The chief root of the trouble is not with the little tyrants, but with our unspanked generation of adult adolescents. Having sown to the wind of permissiveness, we are reaping the whirlwind of domestic disobedience.

How can we hope that parents who as youngsters were thoroughly "Spocked" instead of spanked—how can we expect, I ask, such parents to turn, as if by mental magic, into practical disciplinarians when they have never believed in discipline, either for themselves or for their children?

As commendable as it was for Dr. Spock to confess his former false principles and to admit he is to blame for much of today's "brattiness," he cannot undo the harm done to the present generation of parents, whose inborn bent to unruliness he fostered for years by his foul philosophy of permissiveness. Such parents have become petrified in their permissive ideology, and can scarcely be expected to change.

In contending for a return to practical discipline, we hold no brief for brutality in child discipline, the kind of thing that makes screaming headlines today. We only appeal for a firm, clear and calm control of the child.

Listen to these two inseparables laid down long ago by the All-Wise: "The rod and reproof give wisdom: but a child left to himself bringeth his mother to shame" (Prov. 29:15).

Discipline is the order of God's government for children. Parents are dispensers of it. The child must be conquered, or broken in, to "bear the yoke in his youth" (Lam. 3:27). When reproof succeeds, the rod can be spared (Prov. 17:10). The rod without reproof will not produce a good conscience. But the proper combining of *reproof* and the *rod* will "drive foolishness far away"; it will *"give wisdom."*

John and Charles Wesley, who led the great evangelistic movement in England that saved that land from the French Revolution and millions of souls from Hell, were reared by a God-fearing mother (of seventeen) who laid down some excellent principles for child training (as they appear in John Wesley's *Journal*):

> When turned a year old (and some before), they were taught to fear the rod and to cry softly; by which means they escaped abundance of correction they might otherwise have had. And that most odious noise of the crying of children was rarely heard in the house; but the family usually lived in as much quietness as if there had not been a child among them.
>
> In order to form the minds of children, the first thing to be done is to conquer the will and bring them to an obedient temper. To inform the understanding is a work of time and must with children proceed by slow degrees as they are able to bear it: but the subjecting the will is a thing which must be done at once; and the sooner the better. For by neglecting timely correction they will contract a stubbornness and obstinacy which is hardly ever after conquered.
>
> Whenever a child is corrected, it must be conquered; and this will be no hard matter to do, if it be not grown

headstrong by too much indulgence.... I cannot yet dismiss this subject. Self-will is the root of all sin and misery, so whatever cherishes this in children insures their after-wretchedness; whatever checks and mortifies it promotes their future happiness.

Bible-saturated believers gather this kind of heavenly wisdom and escape the false philosophies of worldly-wise men.

# "Should Christian Wives Obey Unsaved Husbands?"

DR. JOHN R. RICE
answered this question of an inquirer

God should come first with everybody. Wives should put God before husbands, children should put God before parents, and all of us should put God before government.

Or to put it in other words, I think the command to love God with all your heart, mind and soul is more important than the command to love your neighbor as yourself. I believe it more important to love and trust Jesus Christ than it is to pay honest debts, or to quit stealing. God comes first.

But where you are mistaken is when you suppose that you need to break some of God's commands in order to keep the others. You do not need to hate your neighbors in order to love God. A woman does not have to be a poor wife in order to be a good Christian. Children do not have to disobey the command, "Honour thy father and thy mother," in order to serve God. Rather, the more one loves God, the more he or she will be able to keep the other commands of God.

There is not a single contradiction in the Bible. No one has to break a single command of God in order to keep other commands.

Do you think that if women disobey their husbands, they will be better Christians, that more souls will be saved? Of course you and I know that that is not true. Souls are not saved by wives fighting their husbands, or by children disobeying their parents, or by people wronging their neighbors.

So the Scripture expressly says, "Likewise, ye wives, be in subjection to your own husbands; that, if any obey not the word, they also may without the word be won by the conversation of the wives" (I Pet. 3:1). That Scripture says that unsaved husbands who will not listen to the Word, will yet be influenced by and will listen to wives who obey them and that they will be won by the obedience of the wives.

I have known many an ungodly husband to want his Christian wife to go to dances with him or have a drink with him. But I checked up for years and never found a single case but that the wife was a disobedient wife, one not doing what God said about obedience and subjection to her husband. In other words, I found the Bible true on this matter; every wife who will obey her husband, be subject to him like the Bible says, will find that God will put it in his heart to reverence and respect her, and that he will listen to her.

I have never said that a Christian woman ought to go to a tavern with her husband, ought to dance or gamble with him, or curse like he does. That is not my inference. I know that no Christian woman ought do such things. And I know if his wife is what she ought to be, her husband will not command it either.

So where a woman ought to start obeying is on the things that do not violate her conscience, then she will find that she will never have to violate her conscience in obeying her husband.

Again I call your attention to Ephesians 5:24: "Therefore as the church is subject unto Christ, so let the wives be to their own husbands in *every* thing."

Since I believe the Bible is the verbally inspired and infallible Word of God, I honestly do not know any way to make that verse mean something else.

When God says *everything*, He means that. If a Christian woman will simply say, "That is in God's Word, and I will try to obey it," and will trust the Lord for help, she will find that it works wonderfully and that she will never have occasion to do wrong by obeying God.

I believe just as strongly as you do, that every woman ought to love God before her husband and set out to obey God first. But then obeying God will involve doing what He commanded about her husband. Then God must keep His promise and protect that woman and reach the husband's heart, as He promised to do.

I feel that objection to this point you mention will disappear as each individual goes a little deeper into the matter and sees that God Himself has promised to save the husband of an obedient wife. After all, obeying the Bible in this matter will have to be an act of faith, trusting God to work it out.

# No Truly Christian Home Without a Christian Father

## DR. CURTIS HUTSON

The family is the oldest institution in the world—older than the church, older than the state—and in many cases more important than both church and state—because church and state are made up of families. If the home is not right, neither will the church and state be right. As goes the home, so goes the church. And as goes the church, so goes the nation.

If the home is right, then man must be its center. I have seen plaques on the walls of homes that read:

WHAT IS HOME WITHOUT A MOTHER?

But I have never seen a plaque on a wall that read:

WHAT IS HOME WITHOUT A FATHER?

Yet he is the most important member of the family because he is the head of the home.

Mothers are wonderful and they have a very important role to play; but if the home is to be right, then man must be the leader.

I have read another plaque that reads,

GOD COULD NOT BE EVERYWHERE, SO
HE MADE MOTHERS.

It is a sweet sentiment. I know some wonderful stories about good Christian mothers.

George Truett traces his own conversion back to his mother's prayers. He told how he and his brothers saw their mother walk down to the thicket every morning and disappear. They wondered where she went.

167

One morning they followed to see. As they drew near, they heard her pray something like this: "Dear Lord, help me to raise my boys right. And, dear Lord, save them." She called their names. He remembered hearing, "And save George."

George Truett said he looked at his brothers and they looked at him. Then he walked away from his mother's prayer place. But he said this followed him until he accepted Christ.

Hudson Taylor tells of his own salvation experience and tells of his mother's coming home after being away. He said, "Mom, I want to tell you...."

She interrupted: "Don't tell me. I know what it is. You have trusted Jesus Christ as your Saviour. I know when you did it—last night. Son, I was praying for you and somehow God gave me peace that you were going to trust Jesus Christ—and you trusted Him."

He was startled that she already knew.

Thank God for Christian mothers! But no one can have a Christian home without a Christian father. Women sadly know that something is lacking whenever the father is not a Christian.

God depends on men to lead the church. God depends on men to lead the state. God depends on men to lead the home. We need in America some born-again, blood-washed men with a strong spiritual backbone who will begin to lead again in this country.

# Four Ways to Keep Your Husband

## DR. CURTIS HUTSON

Ladies, if you will do four things for your husband, you will never lose him.

1. **Keep a clean house.** Now there is clean dirt and there is dirty dirt. Clean dirt is the cookie the baby dropped thirty minutes ago; dirty dirt is cookies he dropped eight weeks ago and now have bugs on them.

I know if you have children, you can't keep everything spotless, but you don't have to let dirty diapers lie around the house three weeks. I don't know any man who is not frustrated when he comes into a house that looks like a cyclone hit it. We like a clean house.

2. Not only keep a clean house, but **fix good meals.** I feel sorry for this younger generation coming up. Not many mothers now are teaching their daughters how to cook.

One couple got married. The new bride cooked something for her husband. Placing the dish on the table in front of him, she smiled and said, "Two things Mother taught me to cook well: beef stew and lemon pie." The man looked down and said, "Which one is this?"

One may say, "I don't know what my wife does all day, but I sure wish the oven was as hot as the television set when I get home at night."

Keep a clean house. Make good meals—nutritious, colorful, appealing, appetizing meals.

3. **Give him plenty of love and affection.** That's like putting oil in a machine. It makes it run smoother.

One man growled so much that his wife had a nervous

breakdown. Shaking all over, she went to see the doctor. He said to her, "Do you ever wake up grumpy in the morning?" "Oh, no," she said, "not on your life. I let him sleep!"

Well, if he is grumpy, it may be your fault.

Keep a clean house, make good meals, and give him plenty of love and affection.

4. **Don't nag!** No man can stand a nagging woman. The wisest man who ever lived said, "It is better to dwell in a corner of the housetop, than with a brawling woman in a wide house." Solomon ought to know; he had seven hundred wives.

Those four things—keep a clean house, fix good meals, give him plenty of love and affection, and don't nag. "When in the world are you *ever* going to cut that grass? When will you ever learn to hang up your clothes?" Yak, yak, yak, nag, nag, nag will kill a marriage.

I heard of one fellow who joined the army to get away from a nagging wife. She would write nagging letters. He volunteered for frontline duty to get away from the letters, and they would catch up with him, seventeen and eighteen at a time.

Finally he wrote home, "Dear Darling, please don't write me anymore. I would like to fight this war in peace!"

One man's wife nagged so much that when she passed away, he gave a loudspeaker to the church in her memory.

# Does the Bible Discriminate Against Women?

Answered by DR. BILL RICE

**Q.** *The Bible puts the woman in a humble position in relation to her companion. It speaks highly of her as a mother, but children are to be almost totally under the authority of the father. Never or rarely does it mention that a woman is as intelligent as a man and is as able to win over obstacles as well as he. In the Mosaic law the woman is always in second place.*

*Can you give me an answer on this?*

**A.** Let's acknowledge that the Bible definitely does teach that man is to be the head of the home. In the Garden of Eden, after Adam and Eve had sinned, God outlined the basic plan for mankind in Genesis 3:16-19.

*"Unto the woman he said, I will greatly multiply thy sorrow and thy conception; in sorrow thou shalt bring forth children; and thy desire shall be to thy husband, and he shall rule over thee. And unto Adam he said, Because thou hast hearkened unto the voice of thy wife, and hast eaten of the tree, of which I commanded thee, saying, Thou shalt not eat of it: cursed is the ground for thy sake; in sorrow shalt thou eat of it all the days of thy life; Thorns also and thistles shall it bring forth to thee; and thou shalt eat the herb of the field; In the sweat of thy face shalt thou eat bread, till thou return unto the ground; for out of it wast thou taken: for dust thou art, and unto dust shalt thou return."*

Plainly, Adam was to have the responsibility of providing for his family. He was to make a living for them and be responsible for the welfare of his wife and children. Eve was to bear the children and her desire was to be to her husband, and she was to obey him.

Before we discuss the points brought out in your letter, let me remind you that this plan was devised by Almighty God who is not only all-wise but all-loving. *God loves you more than you love yourself!*

And God not only loves you more than you love yourself but He is more concerned for your happiness and well-being than you are. He is more concerned about your welfare. And since God is wiser than we, He knows what is best for us.

Let no one, then, be foolish enough to believe that God has made any mistakes about the way He has planned the relationship of men and women; of husbands and wives. No one can improve upon God's plan.

It is wicked, then, to rebel against God's plan. There have always been children who have rebelled against their parents. I direct America's largest independent gospel camp for teenagers and so I deal with hundreds and hundreds of teenagers just about every week of the summer. And every week we counsel with teenage girls who felt they knew more than their parents and so rebelled against their parents' teachings—and now find themselves pregnant! Almost never does the week go by that we do not deal with this situation.

And every week we deal with teenage boys who have rebelled against obeying their parents and now find themselves in deep trouble because they have contracted a venereal disease or have been taking dope or are facing a possible sentence in a reformatory.

It is certainly true that those in authority can make mistakes or can be wrong, but any preacher who counsels with hundreds and hundreds of people (or any social worker who deals with great numbers of people) has long since found that the happiest, most successful homes are those in which the husband takes the lead and where children are in obedience to their parents.

Furthermore, it is not only wicked but downright stupid to rebel against God's will. Anyone's life will be a far better one if he submits himself to the will of a wise and loving Heavenly Father.

So, make no mistake about it, the Bible does clearly teach that men are to take the leadership in the home.

### Is This Discrimination?

But is this really discrimination? If God's way is best for both men and women, then is this discrimination? Do you really believe it would be better if women generally took the lead in the home?

The fact is, *someone* has to take that lead. Someone must be the pastor of the church, but I do not feel discriminated against because I am not pastor of the church I attend. God has something else for me other than being a pastor. I am not president of the United States, but I do not feel I have been discriminated against because I am not! God has something else for me other than being president of this nation!

I am not pastor of the church I attend, I am not president of the United States, and I am not governor of the state of Tennessee because this is not the will of God for me.

And, dear lady, it is simply not God's will for you to rule over your husband! God has something else for you. This does not mean—not for a moment—that a woman is not as good as a man. It does not mean she may not be as intelligent as he. It does not mean she may not be as capable as he.

But it definitely does mean that God has prepared men and women for the roles they are to play in life. By nature a man is physically and psychologically more fit to be leader, protector and provider for the family than the wife. And a woman is better suited physically and psychologically to be the sweet, gentle, loving, laughing, comforting sweetheart and mother and homemaker.

### Is This to Man's Advantage?

Is this showing favoritism to the man?
I doubt it.

Maybe it would help if I asked another question—Is it better for Jesus or better for the individual who trusts Christ for salvation? There is no doubt but that Jesus wants us for Himself. He wants all men to be saved. But how wonderful it is for the person who has trusted Christ, who has been saved and who does have everlasting life!

Now, God uses marriage as an illustration of Christ and those who believe in Him. Christians are referred to as the *bride* of Christ. And I have never one time heard any Christian say he regretted having been saved. And when husband and wife live according to the Bible, neither could possibly feel discriminated against or ever regret having been married.

In Ephesians chapter 5, verses 22 to 33, we find God's instructions for the way women are to be in obedience to husbands (three verses) and God's instructions for the way a husband is to love his wife (nine verses) and care for her.

Fortunate indeed is the woman whose privilege it is to be the wife of a godly man who follows the teachings of the Bible, and fortunate indeed is the man who has the privilege of being husband to such a wife.

## Does the Bible Indicate Men Are Smarter Than Women?

There may be stories in the Bible about men and women that would indicate that some men are smarter than some women. However, I do not think of any as I write this. But I can think of a number of stories in the Bible where women were wiser than their husbands!

In I Samuel 25 there is the story of Nabal and his wife Abigail. Notice verse 3,

*"Now the name of the man was Nabal, and the name of his wife, Abigail: and she was a woman of good understanding, and of a beautiful countenance; but the man was churlish and evil in his doings; and he was of the house of Caleb."*

This beautiful woman was smarter than her husband, wasn't

174

she? She had compassion on David and his men and she brought provisions to them. It was only then she learned that David had evidently planned on capturing her village, including her husband. Shortly afterward Nabal died and Abigail became the wife of David.

Then there is the story, in II Kings 4, of Elisha and the Shunamite woman. Verse 8 says, "And it fell on a day, that Elisha passed to Shunem, where was a great woman; and she constrained him to eat bread. And so it was, that as often as he passed by, he turned in there to eat bread."

Notice she was called a "great" woman. I believe this is the only one in the Bible who is referred to as "great" in the sense of being a great person.

Her husband is not called great and he did not do anything especially worth recording. But it was the woman who was especially rewarded for her goodness to Elisha; it was the woman who, when her child died, had a servant saddle a mule and who rode to find Elisha and persuade him to come and raise the child from the dead. This lady definitely had more on the ball than her husband!

In the New Testament there is a beautiful story of Mary and Martha and Lazarus. I will not take time to go into the story except to remind you that when Mary anointed the feet of Jesus, He said, "Let her alone; for the day of my burial hath she kept this" (John 12:7).

For the day of His—*what? His burial!*

As far as we know, all the disciples were surprised and bewildered when Jesus was crucified. He had told them that He had come to be crucified, but all of them felt He would surely avoid being put to death. So, when the Lord was crucified the disciples scattered, disillusioned and heartbroken. As far as we know, the one person who had understood that Jesus Christ was going to die—and it is inferred she also realized He would literally rise again the third day—was Mary of Bethany!

Remember, now, Peter and James and John and Thomas and all the others had heard Jesus more often than Mary. Yet she

175

was the only one who realized He was going to die and be buried and be raised from the dead!

Does this sound like God infers men are naturally smarter than women? Does this indicate the Bible belittles women? Not on your life!

## Both Men and Women Need
## to Be Saved

The fact is, all of us, male and female, need to be saved. And no woman is unsaved because she believes the Bible teaches male chauvinism or that she is a woman's Libber! In John 5:40 Jesus said, "And ye will not come to me, that ye might have life." The truth is, an unsaved person is simply not willing to turn to Jesus Christ!

It is as simple as that.

(The late Dr. Bill Rice, founder of the Bill Rice Ranch, was one of the most colorful speakers, had the finest mastery of an audience, gained the confidence of young and old alike, and preached with a tremendous punch.)

# What Is the Best Book for Family Devotions?

DR. BILL RICE

If I were raising my children again, I would use the very same methods we used when our youngsters were growing up.

I would make Bible study and prayer an integral part of our daily lives and I would make talk of spiritual things as natural as talk about the weather. The use of books other than the Bible would be incidental. The reading of the Bible after breakfast was as much of a daily routine as the breakfast itself. The Princess and I and our children gathered with our Bibles and it was understood that this was the time to read and study the Word of God—not a time to talk about other matters.

We read the books of the Bible consecutively, beginning with Matthew. When we had read all of the New Testament we began with Genesis and read every book of the Bible right through to the end of the Book of the Revelation.

Every morning I would begin by reading two verses and explaining or discussing or commenting on them. Anyone who had anything to say about the two verses might speak up. In fact, everyone was encouraged to speak up. Then the next one in the circle read two verses and we discussed them. And so it went on around and around until we had read at least one chapter and often two or three chapters, depending upon the length of the chapters and the interest generated by them. We probably spent an average of about twenty minutes each morning reading and discussing the Scriptures, although we sometimes took more or less time.

Before our youngsters were old enough to go to high school we had read and discussed every verse in the entire Bible. But we had done more than that: we had gone through the New Testament and the Book of Proverbs a number of times.

Let me remind you that this was not simply reading the Bible, but running down references to study what the Bible meant. We read, many times, every verse in the Bible concerning the doctrine of salvation. We studied what the Bible said about the deity of Jesus. We learned what baptism was and why God wanted those who believe on Christ to be baptized. We studied what the Bible says about giving money, about prayer, about marriage, about soul winning, about the kind of parents God wanted their mother and me to be and the kind of children God wanted them to be.

Because the theory of evolution must be faced again and again by our young people, we explained the latest theories taught by evolutionists and discussed the reasons for disbelieving them in the light of Bible teaching as well as common sense.

Long before they were ready for high school, our youngsters were fairly well grounded in Bible truth and their characters fairly well molded.

## "Devotions" Is a Misnomer

Actually, I do not especially like that word "devotions." At least I do not like that word for what I am talking about. When we speak of "devotions" we too often think of a sweet little time together reading a verse from the Psalms and praising the Lord.

Now, I am dead sure in favor of meditation and prayer and praise in our homes. But that isn't what I am talking about right now. I am talking about the fact that the entire family ought to gather at one particular time of the day when everything else is set aside and read and study the Bible and learn how to live in a way that will please the Lord. These family gatherings should be practical, down-to-earth. They should be sensible. They ought to prepare our children for temptations they will meet and decisions they must make.

The kind of "devotions" I am talking about is the kind where the family gathers around the Bible and reads it and discusses it. It ought to change lives. Incidentally, that's why I never recommend these little Precious Promise cards that have a verse of Scripture on one side and a poem on the other. I have been in a number of preachers' homes where the father selected a card each morning at breakfast and read both sides—it takes about 15 or 20 seconds—and then wonders why Junior went wrong when he was "exposed" to the Bible every day!

### Follow Bible Reading With Prayer

Each morning after reading the Bible and discussing it, we would pray together. First, we would discuss what we ought to pray for. Since I am an evangelist and my entire family traveled with me in revival meetings, we were always burdened about the current revival campaign. After the first few days we would know people in the community who were lost and we would pray for their conversion. Sometimes the church would be in a building program and we would pray that church members would give generously. We also prayed for our own financial needs. As a matter of fact, I cannot remember a day in the past 29 years that we have not prayed for money to maintain the missionary ministry of the Bill Rice Ranch. But we prayed for many other things, too.

We prayed that the children would do well in school. Their mother taught them their school lessons everyday. On more than one occasion one of my youngsters would request prayer that he might learn his history lesson because, "If I don't do better, I may get spanked!" (Incidentally, this is *practical* praying!)

We had a beagle houn' dog named Backy that traveled with us. Someone slammed a car door on her tail and she had a zig-zag in her caudal appendage for weeks afterward! Evidently, her tail had been broken. Anyway, it was sore for a long time. If one of the children played with her and happened to hit her tail—she would immediately declare war. Bill III has a little scar on his upper lip until this good day because he ran his hand down her back and hit her tail accidentally!

Anyway, again and again and again one of our children would

179

say, "Let's not forget to pray for Backy's tail." And—again and again—we did pray for that dog's tail in our morning prayer meetings!

Am I joking? Not on your life! I wouldn't have a dog I wouldn't pray for!

Do I really believe God cares whether a hound dog has a sore tail or not? Indeed I do think God cares! The Bible says He knows every sparrow that falls—and any sensible person knows that one good hound dog is worth a million sparrows!

## What About Other Books Other Than the Bible?

There are others I would recommend for incidental use but there is no other book I would recommend using *instead of* the Bible. There are some fine devotional books and I have a number of them. They are good for me to keep on my desk and read a chapter or so during the day. But when it comes to family Bible study, they simply will not suffice.

Now, I said that I would recommend that you begin reading in the Book of Matthew and read the Gospels first of all, then the rest of the New Testament. But I think it might be well worth your while to get some Bible story books and read these stories to your children. Better yet, why not get Hurlburt's Bible Stories or my brother's book, *John R. Rice Bible Stories,* for young and old alike. Read them yourself, then you tell them to your children. In this way, your family will be enjoying Old Testament Bible stories while enjoying and profiting from the study of the New Testament.

# Reckless Spending Problem

### ORD L. MORROW

**Q.** *I have a problem with spending—I'm a compulsive buyer. I buy a bunch of stuff which I may or may not use. I can't seem to stop. My husband and I have some serious quarrels about money.*

**A.** I'm not surprised at all that your problem brings disagreements in the home. If your problem is not solved, it may do more than that; remember, money problems are right up at the top in reasons for divorce. Many people have this problem of spending too much or spending for the wrong things. Maybe we can give a little help for them too.

One thing in your favor is that you at least recognize you have a problem and you know where the problem is. Now the question is, do you really want to stop? You said, "I can't seem to stop," but that really says nothing at all. Of course you can stop! Nothing much ever happens until it reaches our wills. If you really want to stop, there are many things you can do. I will give you a few suggestions, and you can probably think of some on your own. Remember, however, it will not happen unless you really want to stop.

First of all, people must come to realize that improper spending is wrong. Those who are not convinced of that will not stop. People are very clever at finding reasons to keep on doing what they want to do.

What you are doing is wrong because you are wasting money. Isaiah asks a question which you might ponder: "Wherefore do ye spend money for that which is not bread?" (Isa. 55:2). I am

181

aware that there are many interpretations of the parable of the ten pounds in Luke 19, but surely it teaches among other things that we should handle our money with care. As Ecclesiastes 7:12 puts it, "Money is a defence," and it certainly is not to be used unwisely.

What you are doing is wrong because it is causing needless tension ("serious quarrels") in the home. The only strong verse in the Scriptures concerning money is I Timothy 6:10, "For the love of money is the root of all evil: which while some coveted after, they have erred from the faith, and pierced themselves through with many sorrows." Does this not fit your case? Are not your spending habits hindering your faith? Are they not causing sorrows and piercing of heart in your home?

If you really want to stop this foolish spending habit, then sit down and make out a budget for the home. A budget would save a lot of problems and a lot of homes. It may save yours. This means that money is put somewhere for a purpose, and it is put someplace where you cannot get at it when you feel like going on a spending spree.

This means there is to be no undesignated money lying around the house where you can get at it and spend it foolishly, reasoning with yourself that you will pay it back before your husband finds out about it!

This means no money in the purse where it might tempt you. The good word for you is "flee temptation." Just remember that a budget is not something to frustrate you but to free you. A budget tells you what you can and what you cannot afford to spend, and for what.

Why not sit down with your husband and get started on really working something out. Show him you mean business by doing something constructive. Let him know you love him more than you love a bunch of useless gimmicks. It might do you both a lot of good. Don't put it off. Do something about it today. Money is a good servant but a terrible master. Are you content to be its servant or will you arise and be its master?

—From *Good News Broadcaster*

# Working Mother

TIM and BEVERLY LaHAYE

**Q.** *I know of a situation where the wife is pregnant and the husband is starting to go to school. Both are in their middle 20s. You said that a wife shouldn't work and that the first four years are the most important in a child's development. You put a guilt trip on many women who must work in order to make ends meet.*

**A.** Biblical principles give a sense of guilt to those who violate them. If something is right, it's right; if it's wrong, it's wrong.

I don't say that it's wrong for every woman to be working. I did say concerning the situation that you referred to that by the time a child is four years of age, the parents have given to him 50 percent of his potential for learning; by the time he is eight years of age, he has received 80 percent of his potential for learning. So if a parent is going to give a child 50 percent by the time he is four years of age, it means that they will need to spend some time with him. If the parent isn't doing it, it's going to be whoever spends most of the day with him.

No one is going to be as interested in his learning capability or his potential development as the parents. So whether or not both parents work away from home is their decision and responsibility, but it is also their responsibility to see how that child is going to be developed. I think that God gave children parents to help them develop to their very greatest potential. If a mother thinks that she has to work, she must decide what the priority is in the training and development of her child. When she is involved in working away from home during a child's waking hours, she is gone during the best part of the day—the part of the day when she is at her very greatest potential. Probably the time she is at work and is away from her child is the best time for her to be the most patient, the most alert and the most productive. So, it is very important that a parent give a child the very best part of the day she can. At night, when the little child is tucked in bed, the mother is not going to be giving the child any of her best time because he is sound asleep.

There are several other things to consider. Recently, I heard on one of our national TV programs a statement regarding how little a working mother can really gain through her wages after federal, state and social security taxes and, if she is a dedicated Christian woman, Christian giving are deducted. She also has to pay a baby-sitting fee or pay a child care center. There will probably be the additional expense of meals in restaurants, transportation to and from work, parking fees and fuel costs and the need for an increased wardrobe. Perhaps she will need to hire extra help in the home, depending on her situation, and sometimes additional insurance will be required.

When a woman adds up all of these expenses, she may find that the income, if any, will not begin to compensate for the precious time that she could have with her child during his formative years.

The hidden costs are enormous, and I think she has to face reality. The paycheck may temporarily swell the checking account, but people then tend to be more extravagant and the wife will be amazed at how little she is benefiting the family after all.

Another danger that working women have to face involves the qualifications of a working woman and how she relates to her employer. She must be neat and attractive and be submissive to her employer's authority at the office. She must respect him, be polite and appreciative, alert and productive, and be flexible within his work schedule. All of these things are traits of a good business person, and yet they are also the characteristics of an ideal wife. So many times we find the working woman gets the characteristics of an ideal wife and the responsibilities to her employer confused.

And if she is really going to be a good employee who gives total-ly of herself for those eight hours that she is under that employer's direction, she then has to fit those qualifications, which makes it very difficult for her to be equally responsive to an employer and to a husband at home. That complicates things, because the employer may be a good, efficient, hard-driving supervisor, and very dynamic and dramatic in the workaday role but a lousy husband in the home who neglects his own wife and children. So she can actually fantasize a lov-ing, admiring respect for him and actually depreciate in her at-titude toward her husband.

Yes, and unless she is a "super woman," and I dare say that most women are not, she cannot fill both bills. She cannot go to work and be the efficient, capable one that she is trying to be in order to get her paycheck, then come home and be an equal-ly efficient, capable homemaker and wife to her husband.

A woman considering going out to work ought to ask herself, Why am I really doing this? If it's just to have better furniture, better clothes and so on, she will need to see that her children are far more important.

I think women (and men too) should be careful that they never get used to depending on two incomes. Otherwise it will become a permanent way of life. If a wife does need to work, her income should aways be kept separate from her husband's and be used for major bills or tuition payments. The key to every decision in a believer's life is, "Whatsoever ye do, do all to the glory of God" (I Cor. 10:31). Whether or not working away from home glorifies Him is the question for the believer to consider. A mother's greatest responsibility, under God and her husband, is to be a good mother and wife.

# The Wife Who Belittles Her Husband

RICHARD D. DOBBINS, Ph.D.

A licensed psychologist with a doctoral degree in counseling

**Q.** *We have been out with a couple and been embarrassed by the way the wife corrects or belittles her husband. Why do some women seem to continually cut down their husbands in public?*

**A.** First of all, common courtesy makes no room for a husband or a wife to criticize each other in public. There is nothing that is more humiliating or detrimental to marriage.

Why would a person do this sort of thing? A woman may do this because she cannot accept her husband for what he is. She is embarrassed for him in public.

But when she attempts to correct behavior to meet her requirements for acceptability, she fails to realize that her public correction is usually far more obnoxious than the behavior she is attempting to alter in her husband.

In some cases a woman may do this to assert her influence over her husband. This may be her way of announcing who runs the family. Isn't it strange that when she does this, she is unaware of the sympathy she creates for her husband and the hostility she provokes toward herself?

Probably the most prevalent root of this sort of behavior is a woman's inability to accept a submissive role in relationship to her husband.

Many marriages suffer from severe struggles for power. If a girl has grown up in a home where the father shows little respect for the mother and tends to ruthlessly dominate her, the girl may sense a growing determination never to let any man do to her what she has seen her father do to her mother.

This kind of smoldering hostility towards the submissive role of womanhood that is still very much a part of the American marriage scene may make a woman like a short-fused powder keg ready to explode in opposition to her husband, regardless of where they are or with whom they are.

The Scriptures admonish the husband to love his wife as Christ loved the church. If a woman has a husband who loves her deeply and expresses that love in the way he provides for her and the affection he gives her, she should respect him.

Even if he doesn't measure up to these qualifications, trying to make him what she wants him to be by bawling him out in public is like trying to make a child happy by spanking him for being sad.

# "My Husband and I Seldom Speak"

Counseling by ORD L. MORROW

**Q.** *We have been married for over 40 years yet my husband and I seem to be growing farther apart every day. We seldom speak. If I try to talk things out, it just makes things worse. He keeps saying he is going to leave. We are both active in church and I feel this is wrong when things are as they are at home. I've said I will not give him a divorce: am I wrong?*

**A.** To start where you ended, no I do not think you are wrong on the point of not wanting to grant a divorce. It seems to me that the Scriptures are clear on this point, "For the woman which hath an husband is bound by the law to her husband so long as he liveth" (Rom. 7:2). "And unto the married I command, yet not I, but the Lord, Let not the wife depart from her husband" (I Cor. 7:10).

One reason I have chosen to write on this question is that a great many older marriages appear to be breaking up. I'm reminded of what Jesus said, as we read in Matthew 24:12: "And because iniquity shall abound, the love of many shall wax cold." I have no doubt that the love spoken of here is love for God, yet a loss of love for God brings with it a multitude of side effects. It is easy to fall into the spirit of the age, and the spirit of this present age is not one that helps to hold a home together. Even Christian people, if they are not watchful, may find themselves thinking and acting in the same way everyone else thinks and acts. If individuals read and listen to what this world system has to offer, there is no telling what strange things they may be tempted to do.

After 40 years it is not likely to be some big thing that is driving a wedge between you—it is likely to be a buildup of several little things. Little things have a habit of growing into something all out of proportion when married couples allow themselves to grow unhappy with one another. They must find the wedge, or wedges, and work at removing them.

One thing about married life is that couples generally, and almost naturally, do the wrong thing to make things go right. They want the other partner to change. They say that their spouse should see his failures and faults since they see them so very clearly. The problem is that one cannot change others. The only one a person can change is himself.

Why not forget your husband for a while and take a good look at yourself? Oh, I know he ought to do the same thing, and maybe he needs to do it more than you. But you cannot make him do anything, so start where you can—with yourself.

If you feel it is wrong to be active in church, why not stop? Maybe this is one of the wedges. But be careful you do not stop your activity just to bring him under conviction. Make it clear that you are only doing that which will make you a better wife.

Be honest with yourself; I warn you, it won't be easy. Set for yourself a goal of being the best wife in the whole world. Work at it cheerfully. It may take a lot of work, but saving a 40-year-old marriage is worth a lot of work. Count the cost and be willing to pay it. Think of him first for a while. Don't worry as much about saving face as about saving your family. Read Ephesians 5, I Peter 3:1-6 and Proverbs 31 often—and with meditation.

I am not picking on you—far from it. You are the one who wants to do something, and you must start where you are and do what you can. If one could change others, that would be great. Couples could get along with no problem if that were so.

Deal with your own heart. Work at being all you should be as a wife. My guess is that you will see a great change in yourself and, in time, a change in your husband. In response to your diligent desire, your careful consideration as a wife, and in answer to prayer, your husband may still say, "Many daughters have done virtuously, but thou excellest them all" (Prov. 31:29).

# What Is the Place of the Woman in the Church?

### DR. M. R. DeHAAN

When the assembly is gathered together in a scriptural way, then a woman's place is one of silence so far as ministry is concerned. Three things are forbidden to women.

First, they must not interrupt meetings where the Holy Spirit is at work, by asking questions (I Cor. 14:23-35.).

Secondly, a woman must not set herself up as an authority in matters of doctrine, like an apostle (I Tim. 2:12).

Thirdly, a woman must not be put in a place of authority in the church. The place of authority is given to the man. This is no slight upon the woman. It is simply the recognition of her proper place in nature. It is not a matter of superiority or of inferiority, but it is a matter of order.

Regarding a woman teaching a Sunday school class, this has nothing to do with the prohibitions mentioned above, since such a class does not constitute an assembly of God. I do not believe it wrong for a woman, who has been blessed of the Lord with the gift of teaching, to use her talents in the assembly for teaching other women.

For a complete list of books available from the Sword of the Lord, write to Sword of the Lord Publishers, P. O. Box 1099, Murfreesboro, Tennessee 37133.